Commentary on the Book of John

Claudius Brown

Published by Claudius Brown, 2023.

COMMENTARY ON THE BOOK OF JOHN

First edition. May 14, 2023.

ISBN: 979-8223457374

Written by Claudius Brown.

Introduction

The Gospel of John is one of the four canonical gospels in the New Testament of the Christian Bible. It is traditionally attributed to John the Apostle, although there is ongoing scholarly debate about its authorship. The Gospel of John is distinct from the other three synoptic gospels (Matthew, Mark, and Luke) in its content, style, and theological emphasis.

The Gospel of John primarily focuses on presenting Jesus Christ as the divine Son of God and emphasizes his deity and eternal nature. It explores profound theological themes such as the identity of Jesus, his relationship with God the Father, the nature of faith, salvation, and the coming of the Holy Spirit. The gospel contains a number of unique stories, discourses, and symbolic narratives that serve to convey its theological message.

One prominent feature of the Gospel of John is the series of "I am" statements made by Jesus, where he identifies himself using metaphors that express his divine nature and mission. These include statements such as "I am the bread of life," "I am the light of the world," "I am the good shepherd," and "I am the resurrection and the life."

The Gospel of John also includes several notable narratives, such as the wedding at Cana where Jesus turns water into wine, the conversation with the Samaritan woman at the well, the healing of the man born blind, and the raising of Lazarus from the dead.

Additionally, the gospel emphasizes the importance of belief in Jesus as the Son of God for receiving eternal life. It highlights the role of faith and the work of the Holy Spirit in the process of salvation.

Overall, the Gospel of John offers a unique perspective on the life, ministry, and teachings of Jesus Christ, focusing on his divinity and the significance of believing in him for eternal life.

In terms of location, the Gospel of John is commonly thought to have been written in Ephesus, an ancient city in modern-day Turkey. Ephesus was an important center of early Christian activity, and it is believed that John spent a significant amount of time there.

As for the time of writing, most scholars place the composition of the Gospel of John towards the end of the first century, around 90-100 AD. This is relatively later compared to the other three canonical Gospels (Matthew, Mark, and Luke), which are generally believed to have been written earlier.

Regarding the intended audience, the Gospel of John was written for a predominantly Gentile (non-Jewish) audience, as it contains explanations of Jewish customs and practices. The Gospel also emphasizes the divinity of Jesus and presents a highly theological and symbolic portrayal of Jesus' life, teachings, and miracles.

Chapter 1

John 1:1, The Word Became Flesh.

"In the beginning was the Word, and the Word was with God, and the Word was God".

This quote is from the first chapter of the Gospel of John in the New Testament of the Bible. It is a statement about the nature of God and the relationship between God and Jesus Christ.

"In the beginning was the Word" refers to the pre-existence of Jesus Christ before the world was created. "The Word" is a term used to describe Jesus Christ in the Gospel of John, and it represents the creative power of God.

"And the Word was with God" means that Jesus Christ was in a close relationship with God the Father before the creation of the world. This emphasizes the unity and oneness of God.

"And the Word was God" affirms that Jesus Christ is divine and is, in fact, God. This statement emphasizes the unique nature of Jesus Christ as both fully God and fully human.

Overall, this verse is often interpreted as a powerful affirmation of the Christian belief in the Trinity, which holds that there is one God who exists in three persons: the Father, the Son (Jesus Christ), and the Holy Spirit.

λόγος meanings summary.

λόγος (pronounced "logos") is a Greek term with a variety of meanings, depending on the context in which it is used. Here are some of its most common meanings:

Word: λόγος can refer to a spoken or written word, as well as to the concept of language in general.

Reason: In philosophy, λόγος can refer to reason or logic, and the use of rational thinking to understand the world.

Meaning: λόγος can also refer to the meaning or significance of something.

Principle: In some contexts, λόγος can refer to a guiding principle or governing law.

Jesus Christ: In Christian theology, λόγος is often used to refer to Jesus Christ, who is believed to be the "Word made flesh."

Overall, λόγος is a rich and multifaceted term that has been used in many different ways throughout history.

The Greek term "λόγος" can have various meanings, such as "word," "message," "reason," or "logic." In the context of John 1, it is often translated as "Word" with a capital "W" to signify its reference to Jesus Christ as the divine Word of God.

The opening of the Gospel of John draws on the Greek philosophical concept of the "logos" as the ordering principle of the universe. John's use of "λόγος" suggests that Jesus is the divine embodiment of this principle, and that he is both with God and is God himself. In other words, Jesus is the eternal, preexistent Word of God who was present at the creation of the universe and through whom all things were made.

Thus, John 1:1 serves as a profound declaration of Jesus Christ's divinity, his eternal existence, and his role in the creation of the universe. The use of "λόγος" also emphasizes the importance of communication, reason, and understanding in the relationship between God and humanity.

Jesus as the Creator.

"He was in the beginning with God. All things came into being through Him, and apart from Him nothing came into being that has come into being. In Him was life, and the life was the Light of men".

This passage is a verse from the Gospel of John in the New Testament of the Bible (John 1:2-4). It describes the divine nature of Jesus Christ as the Word of God, who existed in the beginning with God and played a central role in the creation of the universe.

The passage emphasizes that all things came into being through Jesus Christ, and that nothing that exists was created apart from

Him. It also states that in Jesus Christ was life, and that this life was the light of humanity. This suggests that Jesus is the source of both physical life and spiritual enlightenment, and that belief in him can lead to salvation and eternal life.

Darkness Cannot Overcome Light.

"The Light shines in the darkness, and the darkness did not comprehend it".

This statement is a biblical verse from the Gospel of John 1:5, which reads: "The light shines in the darkness, and the darkness has not overcome it." The verse is often interpreted as referring to Jesus Christ, who is referred to in the same passage as "the Word" and as the source of life and light.

The verse can be understood to mean that although darkness represents ignorance, sin, and death, the light of Christ brings knowledge, righteousness, and life. The darkness of the world cannot understand or overcome the light of Christ, which shines bright and illuminates the path towards salvation and eternal life.

Overall, this verse expresses the idea that the power of goodness and truth is stronger than the forces of evil and darkness, and that those who embrace the light will not be overcome by the darkness.

John testifies about Jesus.

There came a man sent from God, whose name was John. He came as a witness, to testify about the Light, so that all might believe through him. He was not the Light, but he came to testify about the Light.

This passage is taken from the Gospel of John, chapter 1, verses 6-8. It describes the introduction of John the Baptist, a prophet who came before Jesus Christ and played an important role in preparing the way for His ministry.

The passage emphasizes that John the Baptist was not the Messiah or the "Light" mentioned in the Gospel, but rather a witness to the Light. The Light is a metaphor for Jesus Christ, who is seen as the source of spiritual enlightenment and salvation.

In other words, John the Baptist's mission was to point people towards Jesus, to testify about His teachings, and to prepare the way for His coming. He was not the ultimate goal, but rather a guide towards the Light, which is Jesus Christ.

Jesus as the Light.

"There was the true Light which, coming into the world, enlightens every man. He was in the world, and the world was made through Him, and the world did not know Him. He came to His own, and those who were His own did not receive Him. But as many as received Him, to them He gave the right to become children of God, even to those who believe in His name, who were born, not of blood nor of the will of the flesh nor of the will of man, but of God".

This is a passage from the Gospel of John in the New Testament of the Bible, specifically from John 1:9-13.

The passage refers to Jesus, who is described as the "true Light" that came into the world and gave light to every person. The phrase "true Light" emphasizes that Jesus is the source of all spiritual truth and understanding.

The passage also emphasizes that Jesus came into the world, but the world did not recognize him. Even those who were closest to him, the people of his own community, did not receive him. However, those who did receive him and believe in him were given the right to become children of God. This means that through faith in Jesus, people can become part of God's family and have a personal relationship with Him.

The passage also emphasizes that this new birth or adoption as children of God is not based on human effort or lineage, but on faith in Jesus. It is a spiritual rebirth that is brought about by God's grace and the individual's response of faith.

Jesus becomes human.

And the Word became flesh, and dwelt among us, and we saw His glory, glory as of the only begotten from the Father, full of grace and truth. John testified about Him and cried out, saying, "This was He of whom I said, 'He who comes after me has a higher rank than I, for He existed before me.'" For of His fullness we have all received, and grace upon grace.

This passage comes from the beginning of the Gospel of John in the New Testament of the Bible. It describes the incarnation of Jesus Christ, who is believed by Christians to be the Son of God and the Messiah.

"When the Word became flesh" means that Jesus, who is often referred to as "the Word" in the Gospel of John, took on human form and became a man. "And dwelt among us" means that Jesus lived among people on Earth, teaching and performing miracles.

"We saw His glory" refers to the miraculous works that Jesus performed, which revealed his divine nature and power. "Glory as of the only begotten from the Father" means that Jesus is the only Son of God, and that his glory comes directly from God the Father.

"Full of grace and truth" means that Jesus embodied both grace, which is the unmerited favor and love of God, and truth, which is the ultimate reality and wisdom of God.

John the Baptist testified about Jesus, proclaiming that he was the one who had been prophesied to come and that he was greater than John himself. "For of His fullness we have all received, and grace upon grace" means that through faith in Jesus Christ, believers receive the fullness of God's grace and blessings.

Law of Moses vs. Jesus

"For the Law was given through Moses; grace and truth were realized through Jesus Christ".

This statement is from the Gospel of John, chapter 1, verse 17. In this verse, the author contrasts the Law that was given through

Moses with the grace and truth that were realized through Jesus Christ.

The Law refers to the commandments and instructions that were given to the Israelites through Moses in the Old Testament. These laws were meant to guide the Israelites in their relationship with God and with each other. The Law included the Ten Commandments, as well as other laws and regulations regarding worship, sacrifice, and social behavior.

However, the author of John is saying that while the Law was important, it was not sufficient for salvation. The grace and truth that were realized through Jesus Christ refer to the message of salvation that Jesus brought. Jesus' teachings emphasized love, forgiveness, and redemption, and through his death and resurrection, he made it possible for people to be reconciled with God.

Therefore, this statement is highlighting the contrast between the Law, which emphasized rules and regulations, and the grace and truth that Jesus Christ brought, which offered a way to salvation through faith and love.

Jesus reveals God's nature.

"No one has seen God at any time; the only begotten God who is in the bosom of the Father, He has explained Him".

This statement comes from the Bible, specifically the Gospel of John 1:18. It means that no one has seen God the Father directly, but Jesus, who is referred to as the "only begotten God" or "the one and only Son," has revealed Him to humanity. Jesus is said to have been in close relationship with the Father, symbolized by being "in the bosom of the Father," and therefore uniquely qualified to explain or reveal the Father's character, nature, and will to people. In other words, Jesus is the manifestation of God's love, grace, and truth to humanity, and through Him, people can know and have a relationship with God.

John 1:19-23, John's Testimony

This is the testimony of John, when the Jews sent to him priests and Levites from Jerusalem to ask him, "Who are you?" And he confessed and did not deny, but confessed, "I am not the Christ." They asked him, "What then? Are you Elijah?" And he said, "I am not." "Are you the Prophet?" And he answered, "No." Then they said to him, "Who are you, so that we may give an answer to those who sent us? What do you say about yourself?" He said, "I am a voice of one crying in the wilderness, 'Make straight the way of the Lord,' as Isaiah the prophet said."

This is a passage from the Gospel of John, which describes an encounter between John the Baptist and some priests and Levites who were sent by the Jews to ask him who he was. John the Baptist, who was a prophet and a forerunner of Jesus, answered their questions by confessing that he was not the Christ (the expected Messiah), nor was he Elijah or the Prophet that was foretold by Moses (Deuteronomy 18:15).

When the priests and Levites asked him who he was, John the Baptist identified himself as "a voice of one crying in the wilderness, 'Make straight the way of the Lord,' as Isaiah the prophet said." This statement refers to a prophecy in Isaiah 40:3, which foretells the coming of a messenger who would prepare the way for the Lord.

Thus, John the Baptist saw himself as the fulfillment of this prophecy, and his mission was to prepare the people for the coming of the Messiah. By proclaiming a message of repentance and baptism, John called the people to prepare their hearts and minds for the arrival of the Christ, who would bring salvation and redemption to the world.

Baptizing without proper authority.

Now they had been sent from the Pharisees. They asked him, and said to him, "Why then are you baptizing, if you are not the Christ, nor Elijah, nor the Prophet?" John answered them saying, "I baptize in water, but among you stands One whom you do not know. It is He who comes after me, the thong of whose sandal I am not worthy to untie." These things took place in Bethany beyond the Jordan, where John was baptizing.

The passage is from the Gospel of John, chapter 1, verses 24-28. It describes a conversation between John the Baptist and a group of religious leaders who were sent to question him about his practice of baptizing people.

The Pharisees were a prominent sect of Jewish leaders who were known for their strict adherence to Jewish law and tradition. They asked John why he was baptizing if he was not the Messiah, Elijah, or the Prophet that was foretold in Jewish scripture.

John responded by telling them that he was baptizing with water as a symbol of repentance, but that there was someone greater than him who was coming. John claimed that he was not even worthy to untie the sandals of this person, who he identified as the Messiah.

The conversation took place in Bethany beyond the Jordan, where John was baptizing people. This passage is significant because it highlights John's role as a prophet who prepares the way for Jesus Christ, and it emphasizes the importance of humility and recognizing the greatness of God.

John 1:29-34, Jesus is the Messiah.

The next day he saw Jesus coming to him and said, "Behold, the Lamb of God who takes away the sin of the world! This is He on behalf of whom I said, 'After me comes a Man who has a higher rank than I, for He existed before me.' I did not recognize Him, but so that He might be manifested to Israel, I came baptizing in water." John testified saying, "I have seen the Spirit descending as a dove out of heaven, and He remained upon Him. I did not recognize Him, but He who sent me to baptize in water said to me, 'He upon whom you see the Spirit descending and remaining upon Him, this is the

One who baptizes in the Holy Spirit.' I myself have seen, and have testified that this is the Son of God."

This passage comes from the Gospel of John in the New Testament of the Christian Bible. The context is the introduction of Jesus to John the Baptist, who recognizes Him as the Messiah, or the chosen one of God.

John the Baptist sees Jesus and proclaims to the people around him that Jesus is the "Lamb of God who takes away the sin of the world." This is a reference to the Old Testament idea of sacrifice, where a lamb was sacrificed to atone for sin. John is saying that Jesus is the ultimate sacrifice who will take away the sin of all people.

John also testifies that he had been told by God that the one who the Spirit would descend and remain upon is the one who baptizes in the Holy Spirit. John had seen this happen to Jesus, and therefore testifies that Jesus is the Son of God.

Overall, this passage highlights the belief in Jesus as the Messiah and the importance of His baptism, which signifies His special relationship with God and His role in saving humanity from sin.

Finding the Lamb of God.

This passage is from the Gospel of John 1:35-42, in the New Testament of the Christian Bible. It describes the beginning of Jesus' ministry and how some of his disciples were called to follow him. John the Baptist identifies Jesus as the "Lamb of God," and two of John's disciples decide to follow Jesus. Jesus asks them what they want, and they ask where he is staying. He invites them to come and see for themselves.

One of the disciples who follows Jesus is Andrew, who then brings his brother Simon (later called Peter) to meet Jesus. Jesus recognizes Simon and gives him a new name, Cephas (or Peter), which means "rock." This passage highlights the importance of personal encounters with Jesus and the role of the disciples in spreading his message.

Finding Jesus in Galilee.

The next day He purposed to go into Galilee, and He found Philip. And Jesus said to him, "Follow Me." Now Philip was from Bethsaida, of the city of Andrew and Peter. Philip found Nathanael and said to him, "We have found Him of whom Moses in the Law and also the Prophets wrote—Jesus of Nazareth, the son of Joseph."

The passage is from the New Testament of the Christian Bible, specifically from the book of John, chapter 1, verses 43-45. The passage describes how Jesus met Philip and invited him to follow him, and how Philip then found Nathanael and told him that they had found the person whom Moses and the Prophets had written about, namely Jesus of Nazareth, the son of Joseph.

In Christian theology, Jesus is believed to be the Messiah, the savior promised in the Jewish scriptures. The reference to Moses and the Prophets likely refers to Old Testament passages that predicted the coming of a savior or Messiah. The fact that Philip and Nathanael recognized Jesus as the fulfillment of these prophecies suggests that they believed he was indeed the long-awaited Messiah.

Nazareth doubts overcome.

Nathanael said to him, "Can any good thing come out of Nazareth?" Philip said to him, "Come and see." Jesus saw Nathanael coming to Him, and said of him, "Behold, an Israelite indeed, in whom there is no deceit!" Nathanael said to Him, "How do You know me?" Jesus answered and said to him, "Before Philip called you, when you were under the fig tree, I saw you."

This is a passage from the Bible, specifically from the Gospel of John (1:46-48).

In this passage, Nathanael expresses skepticism about the idea that anything good could come from Nazareth, a town in Galilee. Philip, who had just become a follower of Jesus, invites Nathanael to come and see for himself.

When Nathanael approaches Jesus, Jesus greets him by saying that he is a true Israelite, without any deceit. This is an important statement because in ancient Israel, honesty and integrity were highly valued qualities.

Nathanael is surprised and asks Jesus how he knows him. Jesus responds by saying that he saw Nathanael before Philip called him, while Nathanael was sitting under a fig tree. This revelation causes Nathanael to recognize Jesus as the Son of God.

Overall, this passage shows how Jesus's ability to see and know people on a deep level can help to overcome their doubts and lead them to believe in him. It also highlights the importance of honesty and integrity in the Jewish tradition.

Jesus Reveals His Identity.

Nathanael answered Him, "Rabbi, You are the Son of God; You are the King of Israel." Jesus answered and said to him, "Because I said to you that I saw you under the fig tree, do you believe? You will see greater things than these." And He said to him, "Truly, truly, I say to you, you will see the heavens opened and the angels of God ascending and descending on the Son of Man."

This passage is from the Gospel of John, chapter 1, verses 49-51. In this passage, Nathanael expresses his belief in Jesus as the Son of God and King of Israel, and Jesus responds by telling him that he will see even greater things than the fact that Jesus saw him under the fig tree.

Jesus then goes on to say that Nathanael will see the heavens opened and the angels of God ascending and descending on the Son of Man. This statement is a reference to a vision that the patriarch Jacob had in the Old Testament book of Genesis, where he saw a ladder stretching from earth to heaven with angels ascending and descending on it. By saying that Nathanael will see this vision fulfilled on the Son of Man (which is a title Jesus often used to refer to himself), Jesus is claiming that he is the one who connects heaven and earth, and that he is the fulfillment of the promises and prophecies of the Old Testament.

Chapter 2

Wedding in Cana.

On the third day there was a wedding in Cana of Galilee, and the mother of Jesus was there; and both Jesus and His disciples were invited to the wedding.

This passage refers to an event in the life of Jesus Christ as recorded in the Bible, specifically in the Gospel of John, chapter 2, verses 1-2. According to the passage, on the third day after Jesus had called Philip and Nathanael to follow him, he and his disciples were invited to a wedding in the town of Cana in Galilee.

At the wedding, the mother of Jesus was also present, and she became aware that the hosts had run out of wine. Mary brought this to the attention of Jesus, who initially seemed hesitant to get involved but eventually instructed the servants to fill six large jars with water and then draw some out and take it to the master of the feast. When the master tasted the water that had been turned into wine, he was impressed and remarked that it was the best wine he had ever tasted, even though it had been produced after the guests had already had their fill of wine.

This event is significant because it is considered the first public miracle that Jesus performed, and it demonstrated his power to turn water into wine. It also showed his compassion and willingness to help others, as he responded to the needs of the hosts and the embarrassment they would have experienced if they had run out of wine. The story is often interpreted as a symbol of the abundance of God's grace and provision.

Water turned into wine.

When the wine ran out, the mother of Jesus said to Him, "They have no wine." And Jesus said to her, "Woman, what does that have to do with us? My hour has not yet come." His mother said to the servants, "Whatever He says to you, do it."

This passage is from the Bible, specifically from the Gospel of John, chapter 2, verses 3-5. It recounts an incident that took place during a wedding celebration in the town of Cana, in which Jesus and his mother Mary were both guests.

At some point during the wedding feast, the wine ran out, which was a significant social embarrassment in that culture. Mary, who was aware of her son's miraculous powers, told Jesus about the situation and asked him to do something to help.

Jesus initially responded to his mother by saying "Woman, what does that have to do with us? My hour has not yet come." This may seem like an unusual or even rude way to address one's own mother, but it was a common way of speaking at the time, and it may also have reflected Jesus' recognition that his public ministry had not yet begun.

However, Mary was undeterred, and she instructed the servants to do whatever Jesus told them to do. Jesus then directed the servants to fill six large jars with water, which he miraculously transformed into wine of the highest quality. This act of turning water into wine is often interpreted as a sign of Jesus' divine power and his willingness to bring joy and abundance to those who follow him.

Overall, this passage is often seen as an example of Mary's faith and trust in her son's abilities, as well as a demonstration of Jesus' compassion and generosity towards those in need.

John 2:6-12, Jesus Turns Water to Wine.

This passage is describing a miracle performed by Jesus at a wedding in the town of Cana in Galilee. At the wedding, the host had run out of wine, which would have been a great embarrassment. Jesus instructed the servants to fill six stone waterpots with water and then to draw some out and take it to the headwaiter. When the headwaiter tasted the water, it had miraculously been turned into wine, and not just any wine, but the best wine.

This miracle is significant because it was the first public miracle performed by Jesus and it demonstrated His divine power and authority. It also highlights Jesus' compassion for the host of the wedding and his desire to alleviate their embarrassment. The fact that the wine was of such high quality also symbolizes the abundance and richness that comes through faith in Jesus.

Furthermore, this miracle serves as an allegory for the transformation that can occur in a person's life through faith in Jesus. Just as Jesus transformed the water into wine, He can transform a person's life, taking them from a state of spiritual emptiness to one of spiritual abundance. Overall, this miracle serves as a testimony to Jesus' divine nature and His ability to transform and bless those who believe in Him.

Clearing the Temple.

The Passover of the Jews was near, and Jesus went up to Jerusalem. And He found in the temple those who were selling oxen and sheep and doves, and the money changers seated at their tables. And He made a scourge of cords, and drove them all out of the temple, with the sheep and the oxen; and He poured out the coins of the money changers and overturned their tables; and to those who were selling the doves He said, "Take these things away; stop making My Father's house a place of business."

This passage is from the Gospel of John, chapter 2, verses 13-16.in the New Testament of the Bible. It describes an event in which Jesus went to the temple in Jerusalem during the time of Passover, a major Jewish holiday. When he arrived, he saw people selling animals and exchanging money in the temple. This was a common practice at the time, as people needed to purchase animals for sacrifice and pay the temple tax with the proper currency.

However, Jesus became angry with what he saw and made a whip out of cords. He used this whip to drive out the merchants and their animals from the temple. He also overturned the tables of the money changers and poured out their coins. He then told those who were selling doves to leave and not to turn the temple into a marketplace.

This event is significant because it shows Jesus' zeal for the holiness of the temple and his opposition to the commercialization of religion. It also shows his authority as a religious leader and his willingness to take action against what he saw as corrupt practices.

John 2:17-22, Jesus predicts his resurrection.

His disciples remembered that it was written, "Zeal for Your house will consume me." The Jews then said to Him, "What sign do You show us as your authority for doing these things?" Jesus answered them, "Destroy this temple, and in three days I will raise it up." The Jews then said, "It took forty-six years to build this temple, and will You raise it up in three days?" But He was speaking of the temple of His body. So when He was raised from the dead, His disciples remembered that He said this; and they believed the Scripture and the word which Jesus had spoken.

In this passage, Jesus had just entered the temple in Jerusalem and found merchants selling goods inside. He became angry and overturned their tables, driving them out and declaring that the temple was meant to be a house of prayer, not a marketplace.

When the Jews questioned his authority to do this, Jesus responded with a cryptic statement about destroying the temple and raising it up in three days. The Jews, thinking he was speaking of the physical temple in Jerusalem, were skeptical, as it had taken 46 years to build. However, John explains that Jesus was actually speaking of his own body as the temple that would be destroyed and raised up in three days.

"After Jesus was crucified and then rose from the dead three days later, his disciples remembered his words and believed that he was the Son of God and that the scriptures had foretold his resurrection. This passage is often cited as evidence of Jesus' divinity and his power over death".

Belief, discernment, and caution.

"Now when He was in Jerusalem at the Passover, during the feast, many believed in His name, observing His signs which He was doing. But Jesus, on His part, was not entrusting Himself to them, for He knew all men, and because He did not need anyone to testify concerning man, for He Himself knew what was in man".

This passage is from the Gospel of John (2:23-25), which describes how many people believed in Jesus during the Passover festival in Jerusalem because of the miraculous signs that he performed. However, the passage also says that Jesus did not entrust himself to these people because he knew what was in their hearts.

In other words, Jesus was aware that some of these people may have been drawn to him for the wrong reasons, such as seeking personal gain or status, rather than having a genuine faith in him. Jesus did not base his trust in others solely on their outward professions or actions, but instead looked deeper into their hearts and motives.

This passage highlights the importance of discernment and caution when it comes to matters of faith and trust. Jesus knew that not everyone who claimed to believe in him had a true and sincere faith, and so he was careful about whom he entrusted himself to.

Chapter 3

Nicodemus Recognizes Jesus.

Now there was a man of the Pharisees, named Nicodemus, a ruler of the Jews; this man came to Jesus by night and said to Him, "Rabbi, we know that You have come from God as a teacher; for no one can do these signs that You do unless God is with him."

This is a passage from the Gospel of John, Chapter 3:1-2, in the New Testament of the Christian Bible. In this passage, a man named Nicodemus, who was a Pharisee and a ruler of the Jews, came to Jesus at night to speak with him. Nicodemus acknowledged Jesus as a teacher who had come from God, because he recognized that the miraculous signs Jesus had performed could only be done with God's power.

This passage is significant because it shows that Nicodemus was interested in learning more about Jesus and his teachings, despite the fact that he was a member of the Jewish ruling class and might have been expected to be opposed to Jesus. It also highlights the theme of faith in the Gospel of John, as Nicodemus's statement about Jesus's signs being evidence of God's presence suggests that he is beginning to believe in Jesus as the Messiah.

Born Again Needed.

Jesus answered and said to him, "Truly, truly, I say to you, unless one is born again he cannot see the kingdom of God."

This statement comes from the Christian Bible, specifically in the Gospel of John, Chapter 3, verse 3. Jesus is speaking to a man named Nicodemus, who was a Pharisee and a member of the Jewish ruling council. In this conversation, Nicodemus had come to Jesus at night and acknowledged that Jesus had been sent from God, but he did not fully understand Jesus' teachings.

When Jesus said, "Truly, truly, I say to you, unless one is born again he cannot see the kingdom of God," he was referring to the need for spiritual rebirth or renewal. In other words, he was saying that unless a person undergoes a profound inner transformation, they will not be able to fully comprehend or participate in the spiritual realm of the kingdom of God.

To be "born again" means to experience a spiritual awakening, a transformation of the heart and mind that leads to a new way of seeing and living in the world. This involves acknowledging one's need for forgiveness, turning away from sin and selfishness, and embracing a new life in Christ. It is a foundational teaching of the Christian faith, emphasizing the importance of spiritual renewal and transformation in the lives of believers.

John 3:4-8, Born Again through Spirit.

Nicodemus said to Him, "How can a man be born when he is old? He cannot enter a second time into his mother's womb and be born, can he?" Jesus answered, "Truly, truly, I say to you, unless one is born of water and the Spirit he cannot enter into the kingdom of God. That which is born of the flesh is flesh, and that which is born of the Spirit is spirit. Do not be amazed that I said to you, 'You must be born again.' The wind blows where it wishes and you hear the sound of it, but do not know where it comes from and where it is going; so is everyone who is born of the Spirit."

This conversation took place between Nicodemus, a Pharisee, and Jesus Christ. Nicodemus was trying to understand the concept of being "born again" which Jesus was teaching. Nicodemus was struggling to comprehend how someone could be physically born again, so Jesus explained that being "born again" means being born of the Spirit.

Jesus is saying that a person must have a spiritual rebirth, not just a physical one, to enter into the Kingdom of God. He explains that the flesh gives birth to flesh, but the Spirit gives birth to spirit. This spiritual rebirth is necessary because humans are born with a sinful nature, and they need to be transformed by the Holy Spirit to become a new creation.

Jesus uses the analogy of the wind to explain that the Holy Spirit moves in mysterious ways, just like the wind, and transforms people's lives in ways that may not be fully understood. In essence, Jesus is calling for a complete transformation of one's life through the Holy Spirit to enter the Kingdom of God.

Teacher of Israel's Misunderstanding.

Nicodemus said to Him, "How can these things be?" Jesus answered and said to him, "Are you the teacher of Israel and do not understand these things? Truly, truly, I say to you, we speak of what we know and testify of what we have seen, and you do not accept our testimony. If I told you earthly things and you do not believe, how will you believe if I tell you heavenly things?

This passage is taken from the Gospel of John in the Bible (John 3:9-12). It describes a conversation between Jesus and a man named Nicodemus, who was a Pharisee and a leader of the Jewish people.

In this conversation, Jesus had just told Nicodemus about the need for spiritual rebirth, and Nicodemus did not understand how this was possible. Nicodemus asked Jesus, "How can these things be?"

Jesus responded by questioning Nicodemus' understanding, saying that as a teacher of Israel, he should have understood the spiritual concepts that Jesus was discussing. Jesus then explained that He was speaking about things He knew and had seen, and that Nicodemus and others like him were not accepting His testimony.

Jesus went on to say that if Nicodemus did not believe what He was saying about earthly things, how could he possibly believe what Jesus might say about heavenly things? This emphasizes the importance of having faith and an open mind to understand spiritual concepts, rather than relying solely on worldly knowledge and understanding.

Jesus is the only one.

"No one has ascended into heaven, but He who descended from heaven: the Son of Man".

This statement is from John 3:13 in the Bible and it refers to Jesus Christ, who is believed by Christians to be the Son of God and the Savior of the world.

In this verse, Jesus is speaking with Nicodemus, a Jewish leader who came to him at night seeking answers about his teachings. Jesus explains to Nicodemus that no one has gone up to heaven except for the one who came down from heaven, which is Jesus himself.

This statement is a reflection of Jesus' unique position as the only one who has come down from heaven to earth. It also emphasizes his divinity and his authority as the only one who can provide a way for people to be reconciled with God and to have eternal life.

Belief in Eternal Life.

"As Moses lifted up the serpent in the wilderness, even so must the Son of Man be lifted up; so that whoever believes will in Him have eternal life".

This statement is a reference to a story from the Bible in the book of Numbers, chapter 21, verses 4-9. In this story, the Israelites had been complaining against God and Moses, so God sent poisonous snakes to bite them as punishment. The people repented and asked Moses to pray for them. God then instructed Moses to make a bronze serpent and put it on a pole, and whoever looked at it after being bitten would be healed.

In the New Testament, Jesus refers to this story as a metaphor for his own crucifixion. Just as Moses lifted up the serpent in the wilderness for the people to look at and be healed, Jesus would be lifted up on the cross so that those who believe in him would have eternal life. The belief in Jesus as the Son of God and the Savior is the key to eternal life.

God's Love for Humanity.

John 3:16-21 is one of the most well-known and significant verses in the Christian faith.

In this passage, "For God so loved the world, that He gave His only begotten Son," refers to God's love for humanity. It expresses the idea that God loves the world so much that He sent His only Son, Jesus Christ, to die for the sins of humanity. This sacrifice is seen as the ultimate expression of God's love and mercy toward humanity.

The verse also states that "whoever believes in Him shall not perish, but have eternal life." This means that those who believe in Jesus and accept Him as their Lord and Savior will have eternal life in heaven after death.

The passage goes on to say that "God did not send the Son into the world to judge the world, but that the world might be saved through Him." This means that Jesus' purpose was not to judge or condemn the world, but to save it.

The verse also says that "he who does not believe has been judged already, because he has not believed in the name of the only begotten Son of God." This means that those who do not believe in Jesus have already been judged and are separated from God because they have not accepted His gift of salvation.

Finally, the passage explains that "the Light has come into the world, and men loved the darkness rather than the Light, for their deeds were evil." This means that although Jesus came to bring light into the world, many people rejected Him because they preferred their sinful ways.

In summary, this passage emphasizes the message of God's love and mercy for humanity through the sacrifice of Jesus Christ, and the importance of belief in Him for eternal life. It also speaks of the consequences of rejecting Jesus and choosing to live in darkness.

Jesus and John's Baptisms.

After these things Jesus and His disciples came into the land of Judea, and there He was spending time with them and baptizing.

John also was baptizing in Aenon near Salim, because there was much water there; and people were coming and were being baptized— for John had not yet been thrown into prison.

This passage is from the Gospel of John, chapter 3, verses 22-24. It describes a period of time when both Jesus and John the Baptist were baptizing people in different locations.

"After these things" refers to the events that occurred in the previous verses, where Jesus had a conversation with Nicodemus about being born again. Following this conversation, Jesus and his disciples went to the land of Judea, where Jesus continued to spend time with them and perform baptisms.

At the same time, John the Baptist was also baptizing people in Aenon near Salim. The reason for this location was because there was much water there, which was necessary for the baptismal ceremony. This is significant because it highlights the importance of water in the baptismal process.

The passage also notes that John had not yet been thrown into prison, which implies that this was a period of time before his arrest and eventual execution by King Herod. This detail helps to provide context for the events that are described in the following chapters of the Gospel of John.

John's Disciples Report.

Therefore there arose a discussion on the part of John's disciples with a Jew about purification. And they came to John and said to him, "Rabbi, He who was with you beyond the Jordan, to whom you have testified, behold, He is baptizing and all are coming to Him."

This passage comes from the Gospel of John, chapter 3, verses 25-26. It describes a conversation between John the Baptist and his disciples regarding a dispute over purification practices between John's disciples and a Jew. The passage then goes on to describe how John's disciples express concern that people are beginning to follow Jesus, who had been baptized by John, and they report this to John.

The passage suggests that there may have been some tension or competition between John the Baptist and Jesus, or at least between their respective followers. John's disciples may have been concerned that Jesus' growing popularity could diminish their own influence, and this may have prompted their report to John.

Overall, the passage highlights the complex social and religious dynamics of the time, and the various factions and disagreements that existed among different groups. It also suggests that John the Baptist played an important role in preparing the way for Jesus, but that his disciples may not have fully understood the significance of Jesus' mission.

John testifies about Jesus.

In John 3:27-36, John the Baptist is a prophet who prepared the way for Jesus Christ. In this passage, John acknowledges that everything he has and everything he is able to do comes from God. He also confirms that he is not the Christ, but rather the one sent ahead of Him. John then uses a metaphor of a wedding to describe Jesus as the bridegroom and himself as the friend of the bridegroom, rejoicing in the bridegroom's voice. John says that his joy is made full because of Jesus.

John then declares that Jesus must increase while he must decrease, emphasizing that Jesus is above all because He comes from heaven and testifies to what He has seen and heard from God. John confirms that those who receive Jesus' testimony acknowledge that God is true. He states that Jesus speaks the words of God because God has given Him the Spirit without measure. John ends the passage by stating that the Father loves the Son and has given Him all things into His hand. He also confirms that those who believe in the Son have eternal life, but those who do not obey Him will not see life, and the wrath of God will remain upon them.

Chapter 4

Jesus leaves Judea.

herefore when the Lord knew that the Pharisees had heard that Jesus was making and baptizing more disciples than John (although Jesus Himself was not baptizing, but His disciples were), He left Judea and went away again into Galilee.

This passage is from the New Testament of the Bible, specifically from the Gospel of John, chapter 4, verses 1-3. The passage describes Jesus leaving Judea and traveling to Galilee because he heard that the Pharisees had learned that he was baptizing more disciples than John the Baptist. The passage also notes that Jesus himself was not doing the baptizing, but rather his disciples were.

The Pharisees were a group of Jewish religious leaders who were often critical of Jesus and his teachings. Baptism was a ritual cleansing that symbolized a person's commitment to repentance and their desire to follow God. John the Baptist was known for his baptisms in the Jordan River, and many people flocked to him to be baptized. The fact that Jesus was also baptizing and attracting even more disciples than John may have been seen as a threat to the religious establishment, hence why the Pharisees were interested in this news.

By leaving Judea and going to Galilee, Jesus may have been avoiding conflict with the Pharisees, as well as fulfilling his mission to preach and spread his message to a wider audience.

John 4:5-6, Jesus rests at well.

So He came to a city of Samaria called Sychar, near the parcel of ground that Jacob gave to his son Joseph; and Jacob's well was there. So Jesus, being wearied from His journey, was sitting thus by the well. It was about the sixth hour.

This passage describes an encounter between Jesus and a woman from Samaria at Jacob's well in the city of Sychar.

The passage begins by establishing the location of the scene, which is a city in Samaria called Sychar. The mention of Jacob's well indicates that this is the same well where Jacob, a patriarch from the Old Testament, had given to his son Joseph.

The text then describes Jesus as being tired from his journey and sitting by the well. The reference to the "sixth hour" indicates that it was around noon.

This passage sets the stage for the conversation that takes place between Jesus and the Samaritan woman that follows. The encounter is significant because it breaks down social barriers and highlights Jesus' message of salvation for all people, regardless of race or gender.

John 4:7-9, Jesus and Samaritan Woman.

"There came a woman of Samaria to draw water. Jesus said to her, "Give Me a drink." For His disciples had gone away into the city to buy food. Therefore the Samaritan woman said to Him, "How is it that You, being a Jew, ask me for a drink since I am a Samaritan woman?" (For Jews have no dealings with Samaritans.)

In this story, Jesus meets a Samaritan woman at a well while she is drawing water. The exchange is significant because the woman is a Samaritan, and Jews and Samaritans had a long history of hostility and animosity towards each other.

The fact that Jesus, a Jew, asked the Samaritan woman for a drink of water, which would have involved using her Samaritan vessel, was culturally significant because Jews typically did not associate with Samaritans. This interaction demonstrates Jesus' willingness to reach out to those who were traditionally considered outsiders or outcasts, and to break down social barriers.

The passage also sets the stage for a longer conversation between Jesus and the woman, in which he offers her "living water" that will quench her thirst forever, which is interpreted as spiritual fulfillment. The encounter is a powerful example of Jesus' message of inclusivity, compassion, and love for all people, regardless of their background or social status.

Living water offered

"Jesus answered and said to her, "If you knew the gift of God, and who it is who says to you, 'Give Me a drink,' you would have asked Him, and He would have given you living water."

This statement is a quote from the Bible, specifically from the book of John, chapter 4, verse 10. In this passage, Jesus is speaking to a Samaritan woman who had come to draw water from a well. Jesus asks her for a drink, which surprises her, as Jews and Samaritans did not typically associate with one another.

In response to her surprise, Jesus tells her that if she knew who he was and the gift he had to offer, she would have asked him for living water. The phrase "living water" is used metaphorically by Jesus to refer to the eternal life that he offers through belief in him.

Overall, this passage highlights Jesus' message of salvation and the importance of recognizing his identity as the Son of God. It also emphasizes the idea that those who believe in Jesus and ask for his help will receive the gift of eternal life.

Deep Well, Living Water.

"She said to Him, "Sir, You have nothing to draw with and the well is deep; where then do You get that living water? You are not greater than our father Jacob, are You, who gave us the well, and drank of it himself and his sons and his cattle?"

This statement comes from a conversation between Jesus and a Samaritan woman at a well, as recorded in the Bible in John 4:11-12. The woman is surprised that Jesus, a Jew, would ask her for a drink, as Jews and Samaritans had no dealings with each other at that time.

When Jesus offers her "living water," the woman is initially confused, as she assumes he is talking about physical water. She points out that he has nothing to draw with and the well is deep, so where would he get this "living water" from? She also questions whether Jesus is greater than their ancestor Jacob, who dug the well and drank from it himself, as well as his sons and cattle.

Thirsty Woman Requests Water.

"Jesus answered and said to her, "Everyone who drinks of this water will thirst again; but whoever drinks of the water that I will give him shall never thirst; but the water that I will give him will become in him a well of water springing up to eternal life." The woman said to Him, "Sir, give me this water, so I will not be thirsty nor come all the way here to draw.""

This passage is from the Bible, specifically from the Gospel of John, chapter 4, verses 13-15. In this passage, Jesus is speaking to a Samaritan woman who has come to draw water from a well. He tells her that everyone who drinks the water from the well will eventually become thirsty again, but the water he can give her will be a source of eternal life and will quench her spiritual thirst forever.

The woman is intrigued by Jesus' words and asks him to give her this water so that she won't have to keep coming back to the well. She doesn't yet fully understand the spiritual significance of what Jesus is offering, but her request shows that she is open to learning more and seeking a deeper connection with God.

This passage is often interpreted as a metaphor for the spiritual thirst that all humans experience, and the idea that only a relationship with Jesus Christ can truly satisfy that thirst. The living water that Jesus offers represents the Holy Spirit, which brings new life and transforms those who receive it.

Woman's marital history

"He said to her, "Go, call your husband and come here." The woman answered and said, "I have no husband." Jesus said to her, "You have correctly said, 'I have no husband'; for you have had five husbands, and the one whom you now have is not your husband; this you have said truly." The woman said to Him, "Sir, I perceive that You are a prophet.

This is a passage from the Bible, specifically from the book of John, chapter 4, verses 16-19. In this passage, Jesus is speaking to a Samaritan woman at a well. He asks her to go call her husband and come back to him, and she responds that she has no husband. Jesus then reveals to her that she has had five husbands in the past and that the man she is currently with is not her husband.

The woman is surprised by Jesus' knowledge of her personal history and realizes that he must be a prophet. This encounter ultimately leads to her belief in Jesus as the Messiah and her sharing the news of his teachings with her community.

Location of True Worship

"Our fathers worshiped in this mountain, and you people say that in Jerusalem is the place where men ought to worship." Jesus said to her, "Woman, believe Me, an hour is coming when neither in this mountain nor in Jerusalem will you worship the Father. You worship what you do not know; we worship what we know, for salvation is from the Jews.

This statement was made by Jesus to a Samaritan woman whom he met at a well in Samaria. The woman asked Jesus about the proper place to worship God, as the Samaritans believed that Mount Gerizim was the proper place to worship while the Jews believed that the temple in Jerusalem was the proper place.

Jesus replied that a time is coming when the place of worship would not matter, and that true worship would be a matter of the heart and spirit rather than a specific physical location. He also points out that the Samaritans did not fully understand who they were worshiping, while the Jews had a deeper understanding of God as they were the ones who had received the revelation from God.

This statement by Jesus emphasizes the importance of true worship, which is not limited to a specific physical location or ritual but rather comes from a genuine relationship with God. It also highlights the need for a deeper understanding of God and the importance of recognizing and acknowledging the source of salvation.

John 4:22-23, True worship in spirit.

"But an hour is coming, and now is, when the true worshipers will worship the Father in spirit and truth; for such people the Father seeks to be His worshipers.

In this verse, Jesus is talking to a woman from Samaria about worship and the nature of God.

In this statement, Jesus is saying that there will come a time when true worshipers will worship God not just with external rituals or physical acts, but with a sincere and pure heart, in spirit and truth. This means that true worship is not just about going through the motions of a religious ceremony, but about having a deep and genuine connection with God, and offering him worship from the depths of one's soul.

Jesus also implies that such worshipers are highly valued by God, as the Father actively seeks them out to be His worshipers. This highlights the importance of true worship, as it is not just an outward act, but a deep and intimate connection between the worshiper and God.

Worshiping God in Spirit.

"God is spirit, and those who worship Him must worship in spirit and truth."

This quote comes from the Gospel of John in the Bible (John 4:24). Jesus is speaking to a woman from Samaria about the nature of true worship. He explains that God is spirit, which means that He is not limited to a physical body or form. Therefore, true worship of God must be done in a spiritual manner, from the heart and with sincerity, rather than just going through outward religious motions or rituals.

Furthermore, Jesus emphasizes that worship must also be based on truth. This means that worship should not be based on false ideas or misunderstandings about God's nature or will. True worship involves seeking to know and understand God as He truly is, and living in accordance with His teachings.

Overall, Jesus is emphasizing the importance of a genuine, inward, and truthful approach to worshiping God, rather than just going through external motions or rituals without true spiritual understanding and sincerity.

Jesus Reveals His Identity.

"The woman said to Him, "I know that Messiah is coming (He who is called Christ); when that One comes, He will declare all things to us." Jesus said to her, "I who speak to you am He."

This is a passage from the Bible, specifically from the Gospel of John, chapter 4, verses 25-26. The woman referred to in this passage is a Samaritan woman who encountered Jesus at a well in the region of Samaria.

In this conversation, the woman expresses her belief that the Messiah (or Christ) is coming and will reveal all things to them. Jesus then reveals to her that He is the Messiah that she is waiting for, by saying "I who speak to you am He."

This statement by Jesus is significant because it is one of the clearest and most direct claims He makes about His identity as the Messiah. It is also notable because Jesus chooses to reveal this truth to a Samaritan woman, who is outside of His own Jewish community and considered a social outcast.

Harvest Metaphor Explanation

Do you not say, 'There are yet four months, and then comes the harvest'? Behold, I say to you, lift up your eyes and look on the fields, that they are white for harvest. Already he who reaps is receiving wages and is gathering fruit for life eternal; so that he who sows and he who reaps may rejoice together. For in this case the saying is true, 'One sows and another reaps.' I sent you to reap that for which you have not labored; others have labored and you have entered into their labor."

This passage is a quote from the Bible, specifically from the Gospel of John, chapter 4, verses 35-38. In this passage, Jesus is speaking to his disciples, and he is using the metaphor of a harvest to illustrate a spiritual truth.

In the passage, Jesus is telling his disciples not to think that there is a long time before the harvest. Instead, he wants them to look at the fields and see that they are ripe for harvesting. He is using this metaphor to explain that there are people who are ready to hear the message of the gospel and be saved. The disciples are the ones who will do the harvesting, and they will be rewarded for their work.

Jesus goes on to say that the work of sowing and reaping is a collaborative effort. Some people sow the seed by sharing the message of the gospel, while others reap the harvest by leading people to faith. Both roles are important and valuable, and both the sower and the reaper will rejoice together in the harvest.

Finally, Jesus tells his disciples that they are reaping the benefits of the work that others have done before them. They are not the first ones to share the message of the gospel, and they are entering into the labor of those who came before them.

Overall, this passage is a call to action for Christians to share the message of the gospel with others and to be part of the work of bringing people to faith. It also emphasizes the importance of collaboration and the idea that the work of one person builds on the work of others who came before them.

John 4:39-42, Samaritans Believe in Jesus.

From that city many of the Samaritans believed in Him because of the word of the woman who testified, "He told me all the things that I have done." So when the Samaritans came to Jesus, they were asking Him to stay with them; and He stayed there two days. Many more believed because of His word; and they were saying to the woman, "It is no longer because of what you said that we believe, for we have heard for ourselves and know that this One is indeed the Savior of the world."

This passage is taken from the Gospel of John in the New Testament of the Bible. It describes an encounter between Jesus and a Samaritan woman at a well, in which Jesus reveals himself to her as the Messiah. The woman then goes to her village and shares her experience with the other Samaritans, who also come to believe in Jesus.

In this specific verse, it means that many people in the Samaritan village believed in Jesus because of the woman's testimony about her encounter with him at the well. They were so convinced by her words that they invited Jesus to stay with them for two days, during which many more people came to believe in him after hearing his teachings.

The Samaritans acknowledge that their belief in Jesus is no longer solely based on the woman's testimony, but on their own personal experiences with him. They recognize Jesus as the Savior of the world, which means that they believe he has the power to save people from sin and reconcile them with God.

Jesus visits Galilee.

"After the two days He went forth from there into Galilee. For Jesus Himself testified that a prophet has no honor in his own country. So when He came to Galilee, the Galileans received Him, having seen all the things that He did in Jerusalem at the feast; for they themselves also went to the feast".

This passage is a reference to a story from the New Testament of the Christian Bible, specifically from the Gospel of John, chapter 4, verses 43-45.

The passage describes how Jesus left the city of Samaria after spending two days there, and traveled to Galilee, which was his hometown. However, Jesus noted that a prophet is not usually respected or honored in their own country, suggesting that he may have been somewhat skeptical of how the people of Galilee would receive him.

Despite this, the people of Galilee received Jesus positively, having seen the miraculous things that he had done in Jerusalem during a feast. The passage suggests that the people of Galilee were more open to accepting Jesus as a prophet and teacher than perhaps Jesus himself had anticipated.

Overall, this passage speaks to the complex relationship that Jesus had with the people of his hometown and the challenges that he faced in gaining acceptance and respect as a religious leader.

John 4:46-54, Healing a Royal Official's Son.

This passage is a story from the Gospel of John in the New Testament of the Bible. It describes an encounter between Jesus and a royal official whose son was sick and at the point of death. The official begged Jesus to come heal his son, but Jesus rebuked him, saying that people only believe when they see signs and wonders. However, the official persisted in his request, and Jesus finally told him to go home, assuring him that his son was healed.

The official believed Jesus and started on his way home, where he was met by his servants who told him that his son was indeed healed. The official then realized that his son's healing had occurred at the exact moment when Jesus had spoken the words of assurance to him. As a result, he and his entire household became believers in Jesus.

This event is referred to as the "second sign" that Jesus performed in the Gospel of John, and it serves as a demonstration of Jesus' power and authority as the Son of God. It also illustrates the importance of faith in Jesus' ministry, as the official's belief in Jesus' words led to his son's healing and his own conversion to the Christian faith.

Chapter 5:1

Jesus Goes to Jerusalem.

After these things there was a feast of the Jews, and Jesus went up to Jerusalem is a quote from the New Testament of the Christian Bible, specifically from the Gospel of John 2:13. In this passage, "these things" refers to the events that happened prior to the Feast of the Jews, which is likely the Passover celebration.

The sentence is describing that Jesus traveled to Jerusalem for this festival, which was an important religious observance for the Jewish people. The phrase "went up to Jerusalem" is used because Jerusalem was considered a holy city and was situated on a higher elevation than surrounding areas, so people would travel up to the city to attend religious festivals.

Overall, this sentence is setting the scene for a significant event in the life of Jesus, where he goes to Jerusalem to participate in the Passover feast.

John 5:2-4, Bethesda pool's healing power.

"Now there is in Jerusalem by the sheep gate a pool, which is called in Hebrew Bethesda, having five porticoes. In these lay a multitude of those who were sick, blind, lame, and withered, [waiting for the moving of the waters; for an angel of the Lord went down at certain seasons into the pool and stirred up the water; whoever then first, after the stirring up of the water, stepped in was made well from whatever disease with which he was afflicted".]

This passage is from the New Testament of the Bible, specifically from the Gospel of John 5:2-4. It describes a pool in Jerusalem called Bethesda, which had five covered porches and was surrounded by many sick people who were hoping to be healed. According to the passage, an angel of the Lord would occasionally come down and stir the waters of the pool, and the first person to enter the water after this stirring would be miraculously healed of their ailment.

The meaning of this passage is a matter of interpretation and belief, as it is a religious text. However, some people believe that this story is meant to demonstrate the power of faith and the possibility of divine intervention in healing. Others may view it as a metaphor for the importance of being in the right place at the right time, or as a reflection of the human desire for healing and relief from suffering.

Healing at Bethesda

A man was there who had been ill for thirty-eight years. When Jesus saw him lying there, and knew that he had already been a long time in that condition, He said to him, "Do you wish to get well?" The sick man answered Him, "Sir, I have no man to put me into the pool when the water is stirred up, but while I am coming, another steps down before me." Jesus said to him, "Get up, pick up your pallet and walk." Immediately the man became well, and picked up his pallet and began to walk.

This is a passage from the New Testament of the Bible, specifically from the Gospel of John, chapter 5, verses 5-9.

The passage tells the story of a man who had been ill for 38 years and was lying by a pool called Bethesda in Jerusalem. According to legend, the pool had healing properties and people believed that when an angel stirred the water, the first person to step into the pool would be healed.

When Jesus saw the man lying there, he knew that he had been sick for a long time and asked him if he wanted to be healed. The man explained that he had no one to help him into the pool when the water was stirred, and someone always got there before him.

Jesus then told the man to get up, pick up his pallet (a small, portable bed), and walk. The man was immediately healed and did as he was told, picking up his pallet and walking away. This was seen as a miracle, and it is one of many stories in the Bible that demonstrate Jesus' healing powers and compassion for those in need.

Sabbath Rules

Now it was the Sabbath on that day. So the Jews were saying to the man who was cured, "It is the Sabbath, and it is not permissible for you to carry your pallet."

This sentence is a reference to a story in the New Testament of the Christian Bible, specifically in the book of John, chapter 5:9-10.

In this story, Jesus had healed a man who had been unable to walk for 38 years. The man picked up his mat and walked away, but he was seen by some Jewish leaders who were strict about observing the Sabbath, which was a day of rest and religious observance in Jewish culture.

The Jewish leaders objected to the man carrying his mat on the Sabbath, because they believed that it violated the commandment to rest and refrain from work on that day. They saw the man's action as a violation of their religious law and tradition.

This story is often interpreted as a conflict between Jesus and the religious establishment of his time, and as an illustration of Jesus' teachings about compassion and healing, even in the face of opposition from traditional religious authorities.

Healing on the Sabbath.

But he answered them, "He who made me well was the one who said to me, 'Pick up your pallet and walk.'" They asked him, "Who is the man who said to you, 'Pick up your pallet and walk'?" But the man who was healed did not know who it was, for Jesus had slipped away while there was a crowd in that place. Afterward Jesus found him in the temple and said to him, "Behold, you have become well; do not sin anymore, so that nothing worse happens to you." The man went away, and told the Jews that it was Jesus who had made him well. For this reason the Jews were persecuting Jesus, because He was doing these things on the Sabbath. But He answered them, "My Father is working until now, and I Myself am working."

This passage is from the Gospel of John, chapter 5:11-17 , in the New Testament of the Bible. It tells the story of a man who had been an invalid for 38 years, and who was healed by Jesus. The man was carrying his mat on the Sabbath day, which was against Jewish law, and the religious leaders began to question him about it. The man told them that the person who had healed him had instructed him to pick up his mat and walk.

The religious leaders then asked the man who had healed him, but he did not know, as Jesus had slipped away. Later, Jesus found the man in the temple and warned him not to sin again, lest something worse happen to him. The man then told the religious leaders that it was Jesus who had healed him.

The religious leaders began to persecute Jesus for healing the man on the Sabbath, which they saw as a violation of Jewish law. However, Jesus defended himself by saying that he was doing the work of his Father, who was always working, even on the Sabbath. This passage shows the conflict between Jesus and the religious leaders, as well as the power and compassion of Jesus in healing the sick.

Slipped away, according to strong's the Greek word ἐκνεύω means to withdraw from But Jesus withdrew not to avoid danger but the admiration of the people; for the danger first arose after his withdrawal. ἐκνεύω (ekneuō) is a Greek verb that means "to nod" or "to give a sign with the head." It is derived from the prefix ἐκ- (ek-) meaning "out" or "away from" and the verb νεύω (neuō) meaning "to nod." Together, ἐκνεύω can be translated as "to nod out" or "to nod away," indicating a sign of agreement or affirmation.

ἐκνεύω - nod of agreement.

ἐκνεύω (ekneuō) is a Greek verb that means "to nod" or "to give a sign with the head." It is derived from the prefix ἐκ- (ek-) meaning "out" or "away from" and the verb νεύω (neuō) meaning "to nod." Together, ἐκνεύω can be translated as "to nod out" or "to nod away," indicating a sign of agreement or affirmation.

ἐκνεύω in terms of John 5:13

In John 5:13, the Greek word ἐκνεύω (ekneuō) is used in the context of a healing miracle performed by Jesus. The verse reads:

"But the man who was healed did not know who it was, for Jesus had withdrawn, as there was a crowd in the place. Afterward Jesus found him in the temple and said to him, 'See, you are well! Sin no more, that nothing worse may happen to you.' The man went away and told the Jews that it was Jesus who had healed him."

In this passage, ἐκνεύω is not explicitly mentioned, but it is implied in the phrase "Jesus had withdrawn." This implies that Jesus had given the man a sign with his head or a nod, indicating to him to keep quiet about the healing and not reveal who had done it. This was likely because Jesus did not want to draw too much attention to himself and risk being arrested or persecuted by the Jewish authorities.

Jesus' Relationship with Father.

Therefore Jesus answered and was saying to them, "Truly, truly, I say to you, the Son can do nothing of Himself, unless it is something He sees the Father doing; for whatever the Father does, these things the Son also does in like manner.

This statement is attributed to Jesus in the Gospel of John, chapter 5, verse 19. In this passage, Jesus is explaining his relationship with God the Father and how he carries out his work on earth.

When Jesus says, "Truly, truly, I say to you," he is emphasizing the importance and truthfulness of what he is about to say. He then explains that he can do nothing of his own accord, but only what he sees the Father doing. This means that Jesus' actions are in complete accordance with God the Father's will.

Jesus goes on to say that whatever the Father does, the Son also does in like manner. This means that Jesus' actions on earth are a reflection of God's actions in heaven. In other words, Jesus is the earthly manifestation of God's will and power.

This statement underscores the deep connection between Jesus and God the Father, as well as the importance of obedience and submission to God's will in the life of a believer.

Father's love for Son.

For the Father loves the Son, and shows Him all things that He Himself is doing; and the Father will show Him greater works than these, so that you will marvel.

This statement comes from the Bible, specifically John 5:20, where Jesus is speaking to a group of people about his relationship with God the Father. In this passage, Jesus explains that the Father loves the Son and shares with him everything that he himself is doing. Moreover, he assures his listeners that the Father will reveal even greater works through the Son, which will leave them amazed.

This statement emphasizes the close relationship between Jesus and God the Father, as well as the fact that Jesus' actions are always aligned with the will of God. It also highlights the power and authority that Jesus possesses as the Son of God, as well as his ability to perform miracles and other wondrous acts that reveal God's glory to the world. Ultimately, this passage encourages us to have faith in Jesus as the one who is sent by God to reveal his will and purposes to us.

Life-giving Authority.

For just as the Father raises the dead and gives them life, even so the Son also gives life to whom He wishes.

The statement you have provided is from the Bible, specifically from the Gospel of John 5:21. In this passage, Jesus is explaining his divine authority and power to give life.

To understand this statement, it's helpful to look at the context in which it was said. In the previous verses, Jesus had healed a man who had been an invalid for 38 years, and the religious leaders were upset that Jesus had done this on the Sabbath. Jesus then goes on to say that just as God the Father has the power to raise the dead and give them life, he also has that power as the Son of God.

The phrase "even so the Son also gives life to whom He wishes" suggests that Jesus has the authority to give life to those whom he chooses. This authority comes from his divine nature as the Son of God.

Overall, this statement underscores the belief in Christianity that Jesus is divine and has the power to give life. It also emphasizes the close relationship between Jesus and God the Father.

Judgment given to Jesus.

For not even the Father judges anyone, but He has given all judgment to the Son, so that all will honor the Son even as they honor the Father. He who does not honor the Son does not honor the Father who sent Him.

This passage is from the Gospel of John in the Bible, specifically John 5:22-23. It means that God the Father has given all judgment to Jesus, His Son. Jesus has the authority to judge all people, including those who do not honor Him. The purpose of this judgment is to bring honor to Jesus, just as honor is given to God the Father.

The passage also emphasizes that the honor given to Jesus is the same as the honor given to God the Father. This means that Jesus and God the Father are equal in their divine nature and authority. Anyone who refuses to honor Jesus is also refusing to honor God the Father who sent Him. In essence, rejecting Jesus is rejecting God Himself.

Eternal Life Through Belief

"Truly, truly, I say to you, he who hears My word, and believes Him who sent Me, has eternal life, and does not come into judgment, but has passed out of death into life.

This statement is a quote from Jesus Christ in the Bible, specifically in the Gospel of John (5:24). In this passage, Jesus is speaking to the people and emphasizing the importance of hearing his words and believing in God who sent him.

By saying "Truly, truly" (or "Verily, verily" in some translations), Jesus is emphasizing the seriousness and truthfulness of his statement. He then goes on to say that those who hear his words and believe in God will receive eternal life and will not be judged, but will have passed from spiritual death to spiritual life.

In essence, Jesus is teaching that belief in him as the son of God and in God as the creator and ruler of the universe is the path to eternal life and salvation. This passage emphasizes the importance of faith and trust in God and Jesus as a means of escaping spiritual death and receiving eternal life.

Divine authority and power.

Truly, truly, I say to you, an hour is coming and now is, when the dead will hear the voice of the Son of God, and those who hear will live. For just as the Father has life in Himself, even so He gave to the Son also to have life in Himself;

The statement you are referring to is a quote from the Bible, specifically from the Gospel of John 5:25-26. In this passage, Jesus is speaking to a group of Jews and making a powerful claim about his divine authority and power.

When Jesus says "Truly, truly, I say to you," he is emphasizing the importance and truthfulness of what he is about to say. He then goes on to say that a time is coming, and is already here, when the dead will hear his voice and come back to life. This is a metaphorical statement that refers to spiritual rebirth or resurrection, rather than physical resurrection.

Jesus then explains that he has been given the power of life by God the Father, which means that he has the authority to bring people to spiritual life and give them eternal life. This is a central tenet of the Christian faith, that Jesus is the Son of God who has the power to save people from sin and death.

In summary, this passage is a powerful statement about Jesus' divine authority and power, and his ability to bring people to spiritual life and salvation.

Jesus' power over life.

Jesus in the book of Revelation says he has the power of life and death.

In the book of Revelation, Jesus is portrayed as the exalted Son of God and the conqueror of sin and death. In Revelation 1:17-18, Jesus says to John, "Do not be afraid; I am the First and the Last. I am He who lives, and was dead, and behold, I am alive forevermore. Amen. And I have the keys of Hades and of Death."

This statement highlights Jesus' power and authority over death and the afterlife. The keys of Hades and of Death symbolize His ability to control who enters the afterlife and when. This power is ultimately derived from His victory over sin and death through His sacrificial death and resurrection.

Jesus' claim to have the power of life and death emphasizes His role as the ultimate judge of humanity. He has the authority to determine the eternal fate of every individual, whether they will spend eternity in heaven or hell. This underscores the importance of faith and obedience to Christ, as our eternal destiny is ultimately in His hands.

Authority to Judge.

"And He gave Him authority to execute judgment, because He is the Son of Man. Do not marvel at this; for an hour is coming, in which all who are in the tombs will hear His voice, and will come forth; those who did the good deeds to a resurrection of life, those who committed the evil deeds to a resurrection of judgment.

This statement is from the Gospel of John (5:27-29), where Jesus is speaking about his authority to judge the living and the dead. He says that the Father has given him the authority to execute judgment because he is the Son of Man, a title which emphasizes Jesus' humanity and his role as a representative of humanity before God.

Jesus goes on to say that there will be a time when all who are in the tombs will hear his voice and come forth. This refers to the belief in the resurrection of the dead, which is a central tenet of Christian faith. According to this belief, after death, the body will be resurrected, and the soul will be judged by God. Those who have done good deeds will be resurrected to eternal life, while those who have committed evil deeds will be resurrected to judgment.

This passage emphasizes the idea that Jesus has been given the authority to judge all people, and that his judgment will be based on their deeds. It also underscores the belief in the resurrection of the dead and the importance of living a life that is pleasing to God.

Jesus' Submission to God.

"I can do nothing on My own initiative. As I hear, I judge; and My judgment is just, because I do not seek My own will, but the will of Him who sent Me.

This statement is from the Bible, specifically from the Gospel of John 5:30, where Jesus is speaking about His relationship with God the Father.

In this statement, Jesus is emphasizing that He does not act independently or selfishly but only according to God's will. He says that He cannot do anything on His own initiative, but only as He hears from God the Father. He is highlighting His complete obedience and submission to God's authority, and His actions are based solely on what He hears from God.

Jesus further emphasizes that His judgment is just because it is not based on His own desires or preferences but on God's will. By seeking the will of God the Father, Jesus is able to make righteous and fair judgments.

Overall, this statement reflects Jesus' deep humility and reliance on God the Father. It also teaches us the importance of seeking and submitting to God's will in our own lives.

Jesus explains testimony truth.

"If I alone testify about Myself, My testimony is not true. There is another who testifies of Me, and I know that the testimony which He gives about Me is true.

This quote is from the Bible, specifically from the book of John, chapter 5, verses 31-32. In this passage, Jesus is speaking and he is explaining that if he were to testify about himself alone, his testimony would not be considered true or reliable.

He is emphasizing the importance of having corroborating witnesses to verify the truth of his statements. In the next sentence, he states that there is another witness who testifies on his behalf, which he identifies as God.

Jesus is essentially saying that his own testimony, without any other witnesses to back it up, would not be enough to establish the truth of his claims. However, since God also testifies on his behalf, he knows that his testimony is true and can be trusted.

Jesus explains testimony truth.

"If I alone testify about Myself, My testimony is not true. There is another who testifies of Me, and I know that the testimony which He gives about Me is true.

This quote is from the Bible, specifically from the book of John, chapter 5, verses 31-32. In this passage, Jesus is speaking and he is explaining that if he were to testify about himself alone, his testimony would not be considered true or reliable.

He is emphasizing the importance of having corroborating witnesses to verify the truth of his statements. In the next sentence, he states that there is another witness who testifies on his behalf, which he identifies as God.

Jesus is essentially saying that his own testimony, without any other witnesses to back it up, would not be enough to establish the truth of his claims. However, since God also testifies on his behalf, he knows that his testimony is true and can be trusted.

God said that Jesus is his son

In the Bible, specifically in the New Testament, God is recorded as saying that Jesus is his son. This is a central belief of the Christian faith, that Jesus is the Son of God, who was sent to Earth to save humanity from sin.

The most well-known instance of God referring to Jesus as his son is at Jesus' baptism, where a voice from heaven says, "This is my beloved Son, with whom I am well pleased" (Matthew 3:17). This event is seen as a powerful confirmation of Jesus' divine nature and mission.

Throughout the New Testament, there are also many other references to Jesus as the Son of God, and this belief has been a foundational tenet of Christian theology for centuries.

God called his son God

John 5:31-32. In Christian theology, Jesus Christ is often referred to as the Son of God, but it's important to note that this doesn't necessarily mean that he is God in the same way that the Father is God. Rather, the concept of the Trinity teaches that there is one God who exists in three distinct persons: the Father, the Son (Jesus Christ), and the Holy Spirit. Each person of the Trinity is fully God, yet they are distinct from one another in their roles and relationships to each other.

So while it's true that Jesus is often referred to as God's son, this doesn't mean that he is a lesser or separate God. Rather, he is the second person of the Trinity, fully God and equal to the Father in power and glory. This is a central doctrine of Christian faith and is rooted in the teachings of the Bible.

Glorify Me with Glory.

Jesus said to his father glorify me with the glory which he had with him before the world was.

The statement is a partial quote from the Bible. The full passage is found in John 17:5 and reads as follows (from the New International Version translation):

"And now, Father, glorify me in your presence with the glory I had with you before the world began."

This verse is part of a prayer that Jesus is offering to God the Father, shortly before he is arrested and crucified. In this prayer, Jesus is asking the Father to glorify him so that he may glorify the Father. He is also affirming his belief that he existed with the Father before the world began, and that he will return to the Father after completing his mission on Earth.

This passage is significant for many Christians as it highlights the divine nature of Jesus and his relationship with God the Father. It is also seen as a reminder that Jesus' mission on Earth was part of a larger plan that had been established from the beginning of time.

Divine testimony over human.

Jesus says, You have sent to John, and he has testified to the truth. But the testimony which I receive is not from man, but I say these things so that you may be saved. He was the lamp that was burning and was shining and you were willing to rejoice for a while in his light.

This statement is found in the Gospel of John, chapter 5:33-35, where Jesus is speaking to the Jewish leaders who were questioning his authority. Jesus is referring to John the Baptist, who had testified about Jesus as the Messiah.

Jesus is essentially saying that John's testimony about him was true, but that he has an even greater testimony about himself that comes from God the Father. Jesus is not relying on human testimony to support his claims, but rather on the divine testimony that comes from the Father.

The reference to John being a "lamp that was burning and shining" is a metaphor for John's role as a witness to Jesus. John's testimony pointed people to Jesus and helped prepare them for his coming. However, Jesus is saying that the Jewish leaders were only willing to rejoice in John's light for a short time, and were not willing to accept the greater light that came with Jesus himself.

In essence, Jesus is calling out the Jewish leaders for their lack of faith in him, despite the testimony of John and the signs and miracles that Jesus had performed. He is urging them to believe in him and be saved, rather than just rejoicing in the temporary light of John's testimony.

Jesus' Works Testify.

What it means, But the testimony which I have is greater than the testimony of John; for the works which the Father has given Me to accomplish—the very works that I do—testify about Me, that the Father has sent Me.

This statement comes from the Bible, specifically John 5:36. In this passage, Jesus is responding to the criticism of some Jewish religious leaders who are questioning his authority and claims about himself. Jesus is arguing that he has evidence to support his claims, and that evidence is the works he has been doing.

The "testimony" that Jesus is referring to is the evidence that supports his claims about himself. He is saying that the evidence provided by his works is greater than the testimony of John the Baptist, who had previously testified about Jesus.

The "works" that Jesus refers to are the miracles he has performed, such as healing the sick, casting out demons, and feeding the hungry. He is saying that these works are a sign that he has been sent by the Father, meaning God. In other words, Jesus is claiming that the miraculous things he has been doing are evidence of his divine mission and authority.

Faith in Jesus

"And the Father who sent Me, He has testified of Me. You have neither heard His voice at any time nor seen His form. You do not have His word abiding in you, for you do not believe Him whom He sent".

This statement comes from the Bible, specifically from the Gospel of John (5:37-38). In this passage, Jesus is speaking to a group of people who were questioning his authority and his relationship to God.

The statement means that God the Father has testified about Jesus and confirmed his authority, but the people who were questioning him did not believe in him or have faith in him. Jesus is telling them that they do not have a relationship with God because they do not believe in the one that God has sent (i.e., Jesus).

The statement also suggests that the people who were questioning Jesus did not have a personal relationship with God, as they had not heard God's voice or seen God's form. Furthermore, Jesus implies that these people do not have God's word (i.e., his teachings and commandments) abiding in them, because they do not believe in him as the one whom God has sent.

Overall, Jesus is using this statement to emphasize the importance of faith in God and in his teachings, and to challenge the beliefs and attitudes of those who were questioning his authority.

Scriptures testify about Jesus.

"You search the Scriptures because you think that in them you have eternal life; it is these that testify about Me; and you are unwilling to come to Me so that you may have life".

This statement comes from the Gospel of John in the New Testament, where Jesus is speaking to a group of religious leaders who had been questioning him about his authority and teachings.

When Jesus says, "You search the Scriptures because you think that in them you have eternal life," he is referring to the fact that these religious leaders were very knowledgeable about the Jewish

Scriptures (what Christians call the Old Testament), and they believed that by studying and following these Scriptures, they could earn eternal life.

However, Jesus goes on to say, "It is these [Scriptures] that testify about Me." He is telling the religious leaders that the Scriptures they had been studying and memorizing all their lives were actually pointing to him as the true source of eternal life.

Finally, Jesus adds, "and you are unwilling to come to Me so that you may have life." He is pointing out that despite their extensive knowledge of the Scriptures, these religious leaders were still missing the most important point: that he was the Messiah, the promised Savior, and the only way to eternal life. Instead, they were rejecting him and refusing to believe in him.

Overall, Jesus is using this statement to challenge the religious leaders to rethink their understanding of the Scriptures and to recognize him as the true source of eternal life.

No Love of God.

"I do not receive glory from men; but I know you, that you do not have the love of God in yourselves".

This statement appears in the Bible, in the book of John, chapter 5, verse 41-42. In this passage, Jesus is addressing the Jewish leaders who are criticizing him for healing a man on the Sabbath day. Jesus is explaining that his actions are not meant to bring him personal glory or honor, but rather to glorify God and demonstrate his love for humanity.

The second part of the statement, "but I know you, that you do not have the love of God in yourselves," is a rebuke to the Jewish leaders, who are more concerned with their own rules and regulations than with showing compassion and love to those in need. Jesus is suggesting that their lack of love for others is a sign that they do not truly understand or follow God's teachings.

Overall, this statement can be understood as a reminder that our actions should be motivated by a desire to serve and love others, rather than seeking personal glory or recognition. Additionally, it emphasizes the importance of demonstrating love and compassion towards others as an essential aspect of our relationship with God.

Unbelief of Jewish Leaders.

"I have come in My Father's name, and you do not receive Me; if another comes in his own name, you will receive him".

This quote is from the Bible, specifically John 5:43, and it is attributed to Jesus. In this passage, Jesus is speaking to the Jewish leaders who are questioning his authority and his relationship with God.

When Jesus says, "I have come in My Father's name," he is referring to the fact that he is God's son and has been sent by God to do his will. He is claiming to have God's authority and to be carrying out God's mission on earth.

However, the Jewish leaders are not accepting Jesus' message and are instead rejecting him. Jesus is warning them that if someone else comes in their own name, that is, without God's authority, they will be more likely to accept that person. This may be because the Jewish leaders were looking for a messiah who would overthrow the Romans and restore Jewish power, and they may have been more willing to accept someone who promised to do this, even if they were not sent by God.

Overall, the passage suggests that those who are focused on their own desires and interests may be more easily swayed by false leaders who make promises that align with their desires, rather than those who come with a true message from God.

Seek God's Approval.

"How can you believe, when you receive glory from one another and you do not seek the glory that is from the one and only God?"

This quote is from the Bible, specifically John 5:44. In this passage, Jesus is speaking to the religious leaders of his time, warning them not to put their trust in human praise and recognition, but rather to seek approval from God.

Essentially, the message is that seeking validation and praise from other people is ultimately empty and meaningless. While receiving accolades from others might feel good in the moment, it is ultimately fleeting and dependent on the opinions and fickle whims of others. In contrast, seeking the approval and recognition of God is more lasting and meaningful, as it is based on a higher standard of righteousness and morality.

The passage encourages people to focus on doing what is right in the eyes of God, rather than seeking the approval of others for the sake of personal gain or validation. By prioritizing God's opinion over that of other people, one can achieve a deeper sense of purpose and fulfillment in life.

Jesus will not accuse.

"Do not think that I will accuse you before the Father; the one who accuses you is Moses, in whom you have set your hope".

This statement is a part of a larger passage from the Gospel of John in the New Testament of the Bible, specifically John 5:45-46. In this passage, Jesus is speaking to a group of people who have accused him of breaking the Sabbath by healing a man.

The statement "Do not think that I will accuse you before the Father; the one who accuses you is Moses, in whom you have set your hope" means that Jesus is not there to condemn or accuse the people who have accused him. Instead, he is saying that they will be judged by the very law they have put their hope in and have accused him of breaking. In other words, Jesus is suggesting that they have set their hope in the law of Moses, which they believe will save them, but they are not following it themselves.

Jesus is also pointing out that their accusation against him is ironic because they are themselves guilty of breaking the law. By pointing out that Moses will accuse them, Jesus is emphasizing the seriousness of their own violation of the law and suggesting that they should examine their own behavior before accusing others.

Moses wrote about Jesus.

"For if you believed Moses, you would believe Me, for he wrote about Me".

This statement is attributed to Jesus in the Gospel of John, chapter 5, verse 46. Here, Jesus is speaking to the Jewish leaders who were questioning his authority. He says that if they believed in Moses, they would also believe in him because Moses wrote about him.

In the Jewish tradition, Moses is considered one of the most important figures in their history. He was the one who received the Ten Commandments from God and led the Israelites out of Egypt. The books of the Torah, which are attributed to Moses, are the central texts of Judaism.

Jesus is claiming that Moses wrote about him in the Torah. He may be referring to the many prophecies in the Old Testament that were believed to foreshadow the coming of the Messiah, who Christians believe to be Jesus. Jesus is saying that if the Jewish leaders truly understood and believed what Moses wrote, they would recognize him as the Messiah.

This statement is significant because it highlights the relationship between the Jewish scriptures and the Christian faith. It suggests that Jesus saw himself as the fulfillment of Jewish prophecy and that his message was rooted in the Jewish tradition.

Believing Writings vs Words.

"But if you do not believe his writings, how will you believe My words?"

This statement is made by Jesus Christ in the Gospel of John (chapter 5, verse 47) when he is defending his authority as the Son of God. In this context, Jesus is speaking to the Jewish leaders who have accused him of blasphemy for claiming to be equal with God.

By saying, "But if you do not believe his writings, how will you believe My words?", Jesus is referring to the writings of Moses, the Jewish lawgiver, who testified about him. Jesus is essentially saying that if the Jewish leaders do not believe the writings of Moses, which point to him as the Messiah, then they will not believe his own words, which also testify to his divinity and authority.

In other words, Jesus is challenging the Jewish leaders to examine the Scriptures and to recognize that they point to him as the fulfillment of God's promises. If they are not willing to accept the testimony of the Scriptures, then they will not be able to accept Jesus' own claims about himself.

Chapter 6

Miracles attract large crowd.

"After these things Jesus went away to the other side of the Sea of Galilee (or Tiberias). A large crowd followed Him, because they saw the signs which He was performing on those who were sick".

The passage you are referring to is from the Bible, specifically the Gospel of John, chapter 6, verses 1-2. It describes an event involving Jesus of Nazareth and a large crowd of people who followed Him because they witnessed the signs, or miracles, that He performed on those who were sick.

"After these things" refers to the events that took place prior to this particular incident. In the broader context of the Gospel of John, Jesus had been performing various miracles and teaching the people throughout the region of Galilee.

In this specific instance, Jesus went away to the other side of the Sea of Galilee, also known as the Sea of Tiberias. As news of His miracles spread, a large crowd of people started following Him. They were drawn to Him because they had witnessed the signs or miracles that He had performed on those who were sick.

This passage sets the stage for the subsequent events described in the following verses, where Jesus feeds the multitude with a small amount of food, demonstrating His power and compassion.

Jesus tests disciples' faith.

Then Jesus went up on the mountain, and there He sat down with His disciples. Now the Passover, the feast of the Jews, was near. Therefore Jesus, lifting up His eyes and seeing that a large crowd was coming to Him, said to Philip, "Where are we to buy bread, so that these may eat?" This He was saying to test him, for He Himself knew what He was intending to do.

The passage you mentioned is from the Bible, specifically from the Gospel of John, chapter 6, verses 3-6. It describes an incident where Jesus went up on a mountain and sat down with His disciples. The context is that the Passover, which was a significant Jewish festival, was approaching.

Jesus saw a large crowd approaching Him, and He turned to Philip, one of His disciples, and asked him where they could buy bread to feed all the people. However, it is mentioned that Jesus asked this question to test Philip, as He already knew what He was going to do.

This incident is commonly known as the feeding of the five thousand, which is a miraculous event where Jesus multiplies a small amount of food to feed a multitude of people. The story goes on to describe how Jesus took five loaves of bread and two fish, blessed them, and distributed them to the crowd. Miraculously, the food multiplied, and everyone ate to their fill with plenty of leftovers remaining.

This event is significant in the life of Jesus as it demonstrates His power and compassion. It also serves as a metaphorical lesson about relying on God's provision and trusting in Him to meet our needs, even in seemingly impossible situations.

Miracle of Multiplying Food

Philip answered Him, "Two hundred denarii worth of bread is not sufficient for them, for everyone to receive a little." One of His disciples, Andrew, Simon Peter's brother, said to Him, "There is a lad here who has five barley loaves and two fish, but what are these for so many people?" Jesus said, "Have the people sit down." Now there was much grass in the place. So the men sat down, in number about five thousand.

This passage you mentioned is from the Bible, specifically from the New Testament, in the book of John, chapter 6, verses 7 to 10. It describes a miracle performed by Jesus Christ, where he fed a large crowd of people with just five barley loaves and two fish.

In the story, Philip, one of Jesus' disciples, comments that it would take a significant amount of money to buy enough bread for everyone to have even a small portion. However, Andrew, another disciple and the brother of Simon Peter, informs Jesus that there is a young boy present who has five barley loaves and two fish.

Jesus instructs the people to sit down, and despite the seemingly insufficient amount of food, he blesses the loaves and fish. Miraculously, the food multiplies, and it becomes enough to feed the entire crowd. In fact, there were about five thousand men present, not including women and children, so the miracle was significant in its scope.

This event is often referred to as the feeding of the five thousand and is one of the most well-known miracles performed by Jesus in the New Testament. It demonstrates Jesus' compassion and ability to provide for the needs of many people, even when the resources appear to be insufficient.

Feeding the 5,000

Jesus then took the loaves, and having given thanks, He distributed to those who were seated; likewise also of the fish as much as they wanted. When they were filled, He said to His disciples, "Gather up the leftover fragments so that nothing will be lost."

The passage you mentioned is from the Bible, specifically from the New Testament in the book of John, chapter 6, verses 11-12. It describes a miracle performed by Jesus known as the feeding of the 5,000.

In this event, Jesus took a small amount of bread and fish, gave thanks for them, and distributed them to the people who were present. The passage emphasizes that everyone who wanted to eat was able to eat as much as they desired until they were filled. After everyone had been satisfied, Jesus instructed his disciples to gather up the remaining fragments of food, so that nothing would go to waste.

This miracle is significant because it demonstrates Jesus' power and ability to provide for the needs of a large crowd with a meager amount of food. It is often interpreted as a symbol of God's abundance and provision, as well as an act of compassion towards the hungry and needy. The leftovers being collected to prevent waste also highlights the theme of stewardship and the importance of not taking God's provision for granted.

Overall, this passage showcases Jesus' ability to perform miracles, his compassion for others, and his teachings on gratitude and responsible stewardship.

Leftover Food Amazes People

So they gathered them up, and filled twelve baskets with fragments from the five barley loaves which were left over by those who had eaten. Therefore when the people saw the sign which He had performed, they said, "This is truly the Prophet who is to come into the world."

The passage you mentioned is from the New Testament of the Bible, specifically the Gospel of John, chapter 6, verses 13 and 14. It describes a miraculous event known as the feeding of the five thousand.

In this story, Jesus is surrounded by a large crowd of people who have come to listen to his teachings and witness his miracles. The people are hungry, and Jesus asks his disciples to find food for them. One of his disciples, Andrew, brings a young boy who has five barley loaves of bread and two fish. Jesus takes the loaves, gives thanks, and distributes the food to the crowd. Miraculously, everyone is fed, and there are even leftovers.

The phrase "So they gathered them up, and filled twelve baskets with fragments from the five barley loaves which were left over by those who had eaten" means that the disciples collected the leftover food after everyone had eaten. They ended up with more food than they started with, filling twelve baskets with the remaining fragments.

This miracle was significant because it demonstrated Jesus' power to provide abundantly with very little resources. The people who witnessed this event recognized it as a sign or a miracle and believed that Jesus was the long-awaited Prophet who was prophesied to come into the world.

Jesus Avoids Political Involvement

"So Jesus, perceiving that they were intending to come and take Him by force to make Him king, withdrew again to the mountain by Himself alone".

The statement you mentioned is a reference to a passage from the New Testament of the Bible, specifically from the Gospel of John, chapter 6, verse 15. It describes a situation where Jesus, after performing a miraculous feeding of a multitude with only a few loaves of bread and fish, perceives that the crowd wants to forcibly make Him their king.

In this context, Jesus withdraws to a mountain by Himself alone. His action of withdrawing is seen as a deliberate response to avoid being made a political figurehead or being involved in any worldly power struggles. Jesus' mission and purpose were primarily spiritual in nature, focused on preaching the kingdom of God and offering salvation to humanity through His teachings and ultimate sacrifice.

By withdrawing to the mountain, Jesus seeks solitude and a place of prayer to commune with God, as was His regular practice throughout His ministry. It signifies His desire to maintain a clear focus on His divine mission and to align His actions with the will of His Heavenly Father.

Jesus Walks on Water.

What it means, Now when evening came, His disciples went down to the sea, and after getting into a boat, they started to cross the sea to Capernaum. It had already become dark, and Jesus had not yet come to them. The sea began to be stirred up because a strong wind was blowing. Then, when they had rowed about three or four miles, they saw Jesus walking on the sea and drawing near to the boat; and they were frightened. But He said to them, "It is I; do not be afraid." So they were willing to receive Him into the boat, and immediately the boat was at the land to which they were going.

The passage you provided is a biblical account from the New Testament, specifically from the Gospel of John (John 6:16-21). It describes an event where Jesus' disciples went out on a boat to cross the Sea of Galilee to Capernaum. It was already dark, and Jesus had not yet joined them.

As they were rowing, a strong wind began to stir up the sea, making the disciples' journey difficult. Then, at a distance of about three or four miles from the shore, they saw Jesus walking on the water, approaching their boat. This sight frightened them, as it defied the laws of nature.

However, Jesus reassured them, saying, "It is I; do not be afraid." Upon recognizing Jesus and hearing His words, the disciples became willing to receive Him into the boat. And miraculously, as soon as Jesus entered the boat, it immediately reached the land where they were heading—Capernaum.

This account illustrates Jesus' power and authority over the elements of nature, as well as His ability to provide comfort and alleviate fear among His disciples. It is often interpreted as a demonstration of Jesus' divinity and his role as the Savior and Lord.

Seeking Jesus Across Waters

The next day the crowd that stood on the other side of the sea saw that there was no other small boat there, except one, and that Jesus had not entered with His disciples into the boat, but that His disciples had gone away alone. There came other small boats from Tiberias near to the place where they ate the bread after the Lord had given thanks. So when the crowd saw that Jesus was not there, nor His disciples, they themselves got into the small boats, and came to Capernaum seeking Jesus. When they found Him on the other side of the sea, they said to Him, "Rabbi, when did You get here?"

The passage you are referring to is from the Bible, specifically the Gospel of John, chapter 6, verses 22-25. It describes an incident that occurred after Jesus miraculously fed a large crowd with five loaves of bread and two fish, commonly known as the feeding of the 5,000.

In the passage, it says that the next day, the crowd that witnessed the miracle realized that Jesus and His disciples had left the area. They saw that there was only one small boat remaining, and Jesus had not entered it with His disciples. Instead, the disciples had left alone. However, other small boats from the town of Tiberias had arrived near the place where the miraculous feeding had taken place.

Since the crowd did not find Jesus or His disciples there, they decided to get into the small boats and travel to Capernaum, a nearby town, to seek Jesus. When they eventually found Jesus on the other side of the sea, they asked Him, "Rabbi, when did You get here?" They were surprised to see Him in Capernaum because they had not witnessed Him leaving with His disciples, and they were curious about how He had arrived there before them.

This passage highlights the curiosity and eagerness of the crowd to find Jesus again, as they had been amazed by His miraculous feeding and were seeking further interaction with Him.

Jesus Redirects Materialistic Motives

Jesus answered them and said, "Truly, truly, I say to you, you seek Me, not because you saw signs, but because you ate of the loaves and were filled.

This statement is from the Bible, specifically from the Gospel of John, chapter 6, verse 26. Jesus is addressing a crowd of people who had followed him after witnessing the miracle of the feeding of the five thousand, where he multiplied a small amount of bread and fish to feed a large group of people.

In this context, Jesus is pointing out the motivation behind the crowd's pursuit of him. He tells them that they are seeking him not because they saw the signs (referring to the miracles he performed), but because they were physically satisfied by the miraculous feeding. Essentially, Jesus is highlighting their materialistic and temporary focus. They were more interested in the physical benefits they received, such as free food, rather than understanding the deeper spiritual significance of his teachings and miracles.

By saying "Truly, truly, I say to you," Jesus emphasizes the importance of his message. He wants to redirect their attention from their physical needs to their spiritual hunger and the eternal significance of his teachings. He goes on to explain that they should not work for temporary food that perishes but rather seek the "food" that leads to eternal life, which is the spiritual nourishment found in him.

Overall, this statement reflects Jesus' desire to move people beyond their immediate physical needs and towards a deeper understanding of their spiritual needs and the purpose of his ministry.

Seek Eternal Life

"Do not work for the food which perishes, but for the food which endures to eternal life, which the Son of Man will give to you, for on Him the Father, God, has set His seal."

The statement you provided is a quote from the Bible, specifically from the New Testament, John 6:27. In this verse, Jesus is speaking to a crowd of people who have followed him after witnessing the miraculous feeding of thousands with just a few loaves of bread and fish.

When Jesus says, "Do not work for the food which perishes," he is referring to physical sustenance, such as earthly food that satisfies hunger but eventually spoils and perishes. He encourages the people to seek something greater and more lasting.

The phrase "but for the food which endures to eternal life" refers to spiritual nourishment or salvation. Jesus suggests that people should focus their efforts and attention on pursuing eternal life and the things that have lasting value, rather than solely being preoccupied with temporary and perishable things.

Jesus further explains that he, as the Son of Man (a title he often used to refer to himself), has been given the authority by God the Father. He is the one who can grant eternal life to those who believe in him and follow his teachings. The phrase "on Him the Father, God, has set His seal" implies that God has confirmed and approved Jesus as the source of eternal life and the one who fulfills God's plan for salvation.

Overall, this verse emphasizes the importance of prioritizing spiritual matters and seeking eternal life through faith in Jesus rather than focusing solely on temporary, material needs.

How to work miracles?

Therefore they said to Him, "What shall we do, so that we may work the works of God?"

The phrase "Therefore they said to Him, 'What shall we do, so that we may work the works of God?'" is a statement found in the Bible, specifically in the New Testament, in the Gospel of John, chapter 6, verse 28. In this context, a group of people is addressing Jesus with this question.

To understand the meaning, it's important to consider the preceding verses. In John 6:26-27, Jesus had just performed a miraculous feeding of a large crowd with only a few loaves of bread and fish. The people were amazed by this sign and sought Jesus out. However, Jesus perceived that their interest was primarily in the physical provision of food rather than understanding the spiritual significance of the sign.

So when the people ask, "What shall we do, so that we may work the works of God?" they are essentially inquiring about how to perform the kind of miracles and signs that Jesus had demonstrated. They were looking for guidance on how to replicate the extraordinary works of God that Jesus had shown them.

In the subsequent verses (John 6:29-30), Jesus responds to their question by redirecting their focus from physical works to the work of faith. He tells them, "This is the work of God, that you believe in Him whom He has sent." Jesus emphasizes that the primary "work" that God requires of them is to believe in Him, to have faith in Him as the one sent by God.

So, the question asked by the people reveals their desire to know how to perform the works of God, specifically in terms of miracles and signs. However, Jesus shifts their perspective by highlighting the importance of faith and belief in Him as the central work that God requires.

Faith Over Signs

Jesus answered and said to them, "This is the work of God, that you believe in Him whom He has sent." So they said to Him, "What then do You do for a sign, so that we may see, and believe You? What work do You perform? Our fathers ate the manna in the wilderness; as it is written, 'He gave them bread out of heaven to eat.'" Jesus then said to them, "Truly, truly, I say to you, it is not Moses who has given you the bread out of heaven, but it is My Father who gives you the true bread out of heaven. For the bread of God is that which comes down out of heaven, and gives life to the world." Then they said to Him, "Lord, always give us this bread."

The passage you provided is from the New Testament of the Bible, specifically from the Gospel of John, chapter 6, verses 29-34. In this dialogue, Jesus is speaking to a crowd who is seeking a sign or miracle from Him.

When Jesus says, "This is the work of God, that you believe in Him whom He has sent," He is emphasizing the importance of faith. Jesus is saying that the primary work or task appointed by God is to have faith in Him, to believe in Him as the one whom God has sent. He is highlighting the significance of a personal relationship with God through faith rather than merely seeking signs and miracles.

The crowd then asks Jesus for a sign, referring to the miracle of manna, which according to the Old Testament, God provided to the Israelites in the wilderness during their journey from Egypt. They are essentially asking Jesus to prove Himself by performing a similar miracle.

In response, Jesus clarifies that it was not Moses who provided the bread from heaven (manna), but rather it was God, His Father. He then introduces the concept of the "true bread out of heaven," which is the bread of God that gives life to the world. Jesus is shifting the focus from physical bread to spiritual nourishment and eternal life.

The crowd, seemingly understanding this metaphorical teaching, responds by saying, "Lord, always give us this bread." They are expressing their desire for this bread of life that Jesus is referring to, recognizing the spiritual significance behind His words.

This passage showcases Jesus' teachings on the importance of faith and belief in Him as the one sent by God, as well as the distinction between physical and spiritual nourishment. It emphasizes the need for a deeper understanding of Jesus' mission and message beyond seeking signs and miracles.

Jesus, Bread of Life

Jesus said to them, "I am the bread of life; he who comes to Me will not hunger, and he who believes in Me will never thirst.

This statement is attributed to Jesus in the Bible, specifically in the Gospel of John, Chapter 6, verse 35. Jesus uses the metaphor of bread to convey a spiritual truth to his followers.

When Jesus says, "I am the bread of life," he is expressing that he is the source of spiritual sustenance and fulfillment. Just as bread is essential for physical nourishment and sustains life, Jesus is emphasizing that he is the one who provides spiritual nourishment and sustains eternal life.

The phrase "he who comes to Me will not hunger, and he who believes in Me will never thirst" further emphasizes this point. Jesus is inviting people to come to him, to seek a relationship with him, and to believe in him. By doing so, they will find spiritual satisfaction and fulfillment that surpasses any other longing or desire.

In essence, Jesus is speaking of the deep spiritual hunger and thirst that exist within every person and how he alone can satisfy those needs. He offers himself as the solution to the spiritual emptiness and longing that people experience, promising eternal fulfillment through a relationship with him.

Unbelievers Won't Receive

But I said to you that you have seen Me, and yet do not believe. All that the Father gives Me will come to Me, and the one who comes to Me I will certainly not cast out. For I have come down from heaven, not to do My own will, but the will of Him who sent Me. This is the will of Him who sent Me, that of all that He has given Me I lose nothing, but raise it up on the last day. For this is the will of My Father, that everyone who beholds the Son and believes in Him will have eternal life, and I Myself will raise him up on the last day."

The passage you have provided is from the New Testament of the Bible, specifically from the book of John, chapter 6, verses 36-40. These verses are part of a larger discourse where Jesus is speaking to a crowd of people who have followed him after witnessing the miracle of the feeding of the five thousand.

In this passage, Jesus is explaining his identity and mission to the crowd. He says, "But I said to you that you have seen Me, and yet do not believe." Here, Jesus is addressing those who have seen him perform miracles and heard his teachings but still do not believe in him.

Jesus continues by saying, "All that the Father gives Me will come to Me, and the one who comes to Me I will certainly not cast out." He is expressing the idea that those who are given to him by God the Father will come to him, and he will not reject or turn away anyone who comes to him seeking salvation.

Jesus then explains that his purpose is not to fulfill his own will, but to carry out the will of God the Father who sent him. He states, "For I have come down from heaven, not to do My own will, but the will of Him who sent Me." Jesus emphasizes that his mission is to do the will of God.

Next, Jesus states, "This is the will of Him who sent Me, that of all that He has given Me I lose nothing, but raise it up on the last day." Here, Jesus is affirming that it is the will of God the Father that he preserves and raises up all those who have been given to him, ensuring their eternal salvation.

Finally, Jesus concludes by saying, "For this is the will of My Father, that everyone who beholds the Son and believes in Him will have eternal life, and I Myself will raise him up on the last day." Jesus emphasizes that anyone who sees him and believes in him will receive eternal life, and he will raise them up on the last day, referring to the future resurrection and judgment.

Overall, this passage showcases Jesus' divine authority, his role as the one sent by God the Father, and his promise of eternal life to those who believe in him.

Jews Grumble Over Jesus

Therefore the Jews were grumbling about Him, because He said, "I am the bread that came down out of heaven."

The statement "Therefore the Jews were grumbling about Him, because He said, 'I am the bread that came down out of heaven'" refers to a specific event or passage in the Bible. This sentence is taken from the New Testament in the book of John, chapter 6, verse 41.

In this context, Jesus is speaking to a crowd of people after miraculously feeding them with a small amount of bread and fish. He uses the metaphor of being the "bread that came down out of heaven" to illustrate his role as the source of spiritual nourishment and eternal life.

The response of the Jews, or the Jewish people listening to Jesus, is described as grumbling. They are expressing their discontent or dissatisfaction with his statement. This grumbling can be seen as a form of questioning or disbelief in Jesus' claim to be the source of divine sustenance.

This passage is part of a larger narrative in which Jesus discusses his identity and purpose, emphasizing the importance of faith in him as the means of receiving eternal life. The grumbling of the Jews serves as a catalyst for further dialogue and teaching from Jesus.

Jesus' Divine Origin Doubt

They were saying, "Is not this Jesus, the son of Joseph, whose father and mother we know? How does He now say, 'I have come down out of heaven'?"

The statement you mentioned is a quote from the Bible, specifically John 6:42. In this verse, people were expressing surprise and disbelief at Jesus' claim that he had come down from heaven. They were questioning how this could be true because they were familiar with Jesus as the son of Joseph and Mary, whose earthly parents they knew.

The context of this quote is a conversation between Jesus and a crowd of people who had witnessed his miraculous feeding of thousands with just a few loaves of bread and fish. Jesus used this event to teach about his role as the "bread of life" and the importance of believing in him for eternal life.

The people in the crowd were struggling to reconcile their knowledge of Jesus' human background with his claim to have come down from heaven. They saw him as a mere mortal, the son of Joseph and Mary, and found it difficult to accept his divine origin.

This passage reflects the skepticism and doubt that some people had toward Jesus' claims about his identity and mission. It also highlights the challenge of understanding Jesus' divine nature while perceiving his human appearance and background.

Jesus: Bread of Life

Jesus answered and said to them, "Do not grumble among yourselves. No one can come to Me unless the Father who sent Me draws him; and I will raise him up on the last day. It is written in the prophets, 'And they shall all be taught of God.' Everyone who has heard and learned from the Father, comes to Me. Not that anyone has seen the Father, except the One who is from God; He has seen the Father. Truly, truly, I say to you, he who believes has eternal life. I am the bread of life.

The passage you mentioned is from the Bible, specifically from the Gospel of John, chapter 6, verses 43-48. In this passage, Jesus is speaking to a group of people who were grumbling or complaining about Him.

When Jesus says, "Do not grumble among yourselves," He is telling them not to complain or argue about what He is saying. He then goes on to explain that no one can come to Him unless the Father, who sent Him, draws them. This means that belief in Jesus and coming to Him is ultimately a result of God's calling or drawing individuals to Himself.

Jesus continues by saying that those who are taught by God, as foretold by the prophets, will come to Him. In other words, those who hear and learn from the Father will believe in Jesus and seek a relationship with Him. Jesus emphasizes that no one has seen the

Father except Him, as He is the one who comes from God and has seen the Father.

Finally, Jesus makes a profound statement, "Truly, truly, I say to you, he who believes has eternal life." Here, Jesus is asserting that eternal life is granted to those who believe in Him. He describes Himself as the "bread of life," which is a metaphorical way of saying that He provides spiritual sustenance and eternal life to those who trust in Him.

Overall, this passage highlights Jesus' role as the one who reveals the Father and offers eternal life to those who believe in Him. It emphasizes the importance of being taught by God and draws attention to the significance of faith in Jesus as the means to obtain eternal life.

Eternal Bread of Life

Your fathers ate the manna in the wilderness, and they died. This is the bread which comes down out of heaven, so that one may eat of it and not die. I am the living bread that came down out of heaven; if anyone eats of this bread, he will live forever; and the bread also which I will give for the life of the world is My flesh."

The statement you provided is a passage from the Bible, specifically from the New Testament in the book of John, chapter 6, verses 49-51. These verses are part of a larger discourse where Jesus is speaking to a crowd of people who were following Him after He miraculously fed them with bread and fish.

In this passage, Jesus is using metaphorical language to explain His identity and purpose. He references the manna, which was the miraculous bread that God provided to the Israelites in the wilderness during their journey from Egypt to the Promised Land. Jesus points out that although their ancestors ate the manna, they eventually died. He then contrasts the manna with Himself, claiming to be the "living bread" that came down from heaven.

Jesus is essentially saying that just as the manna sustained physical life temporarily, He is the spiritual bread that gives eternal life. He claims that if anyone eats of this spiritual bread, which symbolizes a personal relationship with Him, they will live forever. He further states that the bread He will give for the life of the world is His flesh, alluding to His upcoming sacrifice on the cross, where He would give His own body as an atonement for the sins of humanity.

Overall, this passage highlights Jesus' role as the source of eternal life and emphasizes the importance of a spiritual connection with Him for salvation and everlasting life.

Eucharist Symbolic Spiritual Nourishment

Then the Jews began to argue with one another, saying, "How can this man give us His flesh to eat?" So Jesus said to them, "Truly, truly, I say to you, unless you eat the flesh of the Son of Man and drink His blood, you have no life in yourselves. He who eats My flesh and drinks My blood has eternal life, and I will raise him up on the last day. For My flesh is true food, and My blood is true drink. He who eats My flesh and drinks My blood abides in Me, and I in him. As the living Father sent Me, and I live because of the Father, so he who eats Me, he also will live because of Me. This is the bread which came down out of heaven; not as the fathers ate and died; he who eats this bread will live forever."

The passage you quoted is from the Bible, specifically from the Gospel of John, chapter 6, verses 52-58. In this passage, Jesus is speaking to a crowd of people, including Jews, and he makes a statement that is difficult for them to understand.

Jesus says that unless they eat his flesh and drink his blood, they have no life in themselves. This statement is metaphorical and symbolic, rather than literal. Jesus is using this language to convey a deeper spiritual truth.

In Christian theology, this statement is often understood to be a reference to the Eucharist, also known as Communion or the Lord's Supper. The Eucharist is a sacrament in which Christians consume bread and wine, which are understood to represent the body and blood of Jesus. By participating in the Eucharist, Christians believe that they are spiritually united with Christ and receive the benefits of his sacrifice.

In the passage, Jesus emphasizes that by partaking in him, symbolized by eating his flesh and drinking his blood, people will have eternal life and will be raised up on the last day. He describes his flesh as true food and his blood as true drink, indicating the spiritual nourishment and sustenance that comes from being in a relationship with him.

Jesus also contrasts the bread that the Israelites ate in the wilderness, which only sustained them temporarily, with the bread that he offers, which leads to eternal life. He presents himself as the "bread of life" that has come down from heaven, and those who partake in him will live forever.

It's important to note that interpretations of this passage may vary among different Christian denominations and traditions, but the overarching theme revolves around the spiritual significance of being united with Jesus through faith and participation in the Eucharist. But Jesus is not talking about the Eucharist because anyone who eats and drink if the cup unworthily, drinks and eat damnation to himself. If you read on you will see that Jesus is talking about believing in him and his words.

Eternal life through bread.

"If anyone eats of this bread, he will live forever; and the bread also which I will give for the life of the world is My flesh."

The statement you provided appears to be a reference to a passage from the Christian Bible, specifically from the New Testament in the Gospel of John, chapter 6, verse 51. In this verse,

Jesus is speaking to his followers and makes a symbolic statement about bread and eternal life. Let's break it down:

"If anyone eats of this bread, he will live forever":

This statement suggests that by partaking in the "bread" mentioned, one can attain eternal life. In a figurative sense, Jesus is referring to himself as the bread of life, and by believing in him and his teachings, individuals can obtain spiritual nourishment and eternal life.

"The bread also which I will give for the life of the world is My flesh":

In this part, Jesus goes further in his metaphorical language by stating that the bread he gives is his flesh. He is using symbolic language to express that he will offer himself as a sacrifice for the benefit of all people. This sacrifice is understood in Christian theology as Jesus' crucifixion, where he gave his life on the cross to redeem humanity from sin and offer the possibility of eternal life.

Overall, the passage emphasizes the belief that through faith in Jesus and his sacrifice, individuals can receive spiritual nourishment and obtain eternal life. It is a central concept in Christian theology and relates to the idea of salvation and the transformative power of faith.

Difficult Teachings Emphasize Spiritual Life

These things He said in the synagogue as He taught in Capernaum. Therefore many of His disciples, when they heard this said, "This is a difficult statement; who can listen to it?" But Jesus, conscious that His disciples grumbled at this, said to them, "Does this cause you to stumble? What then if you see the Son of Man ascending to where He was before? It is the Spirit who gives life; the flesh profits nothing; the words that I have spoken to you are spirit and are life.

The passage you're referring to comes from the New Testament of the Bible, specifically from the Gospel of John, chapter 6, verses

75

59-63. In this passage, Jesus is teaching in the synagogue in Capernaum and making statements that some of His disciples find difficult to understand.

When the disciples hear what Jesus is saying, they react by saying, "This is a difficult statement; who can listen to it?" They are struggling to comprehend the meaning behind His words and find them challenging to accept or follow.

Jesus, aware of their grumbling and confusion, responds by asking them if His words are causing them to stumble or doubt their faith. He then poses a rhetorical question, saying, "What then if you see the Son of Man ascending to where He was before?" This is a reference to His future ascension to heaven.

Jesus goes on to explain that it is the Spirit who gives life, emphasizing the spiritual nature of His teachings. He contrasts the spirit with the flesh, saying that the flesh (physical existence) profits nothing in comparison to the spiritual realm. He further emphasizes that the words He has spoken are spirit and life, suggesting that His teachings hold the key to understanding and experiencing true spiritual life.

In this passage, Jesus is addressing the disciples' struggle to comprehend His teachings and encouraging them to focus on the spiritual aspects rather than being limited by their physical understanding. He asserts the importance of the Holy Spirit in bringing life and understanding to His teachings, indicating that they hold spiritual significance and are essential for true life and faith.

Faith's Origin and Knowledge

But there are some of you who do not believe." For Jesus knew from the beginning who they were who did not believe, and who it was that would betray Him. And He was saying, "For this reason I have said to you, that no one can come to Me unless it has been granted him from the Father."

The passage you provided is from the New Testament of the Bible, specifically from the Gospel of John (John 6:64-65). In this context, Jesus is speaking to a group of his disciples and followers. Let's break down the meaning of the passage:

"But there are some of you who do not believe."

Jesus is acknowledging that among the people listening to him, there are those who do not have faith in him or his teachings. He is aware that not everyone accepts his message.

"For Jesus knew from the beginning who they were who did not believe, and who it was that would betray Him."

Here, it is emphasized that Jesus, being divine, had knowledge of the hearts and intentions of those present. He knew beforehand which individuals would not believe in him and even who would ultimately betray him. This highlights Jesus' divine insight and foreknowledge.

"And He was saying, 'For this reason I have said to you, that no one can come to Me unless it has been granted him from the Father.'"

Jesus explains that the reason he mentioned the disbelief and betrayal is to make a broader point about faith. He asserts that the ability to come to him and believe in him is not something that can be achieved by mere human will or effort. Instead, it is granted by the Father, referring to God. Jesus suggests that faith is a gift from God and that individuals can only come to him if God allows and enables it.

In summary, Jesus acknowledges the presence of non-believers among his listeners, knowing their identities and even the one who would betray him. He uses this as an opportunity to emphasize that faith is not solely a result of human choice but is granted by God.

Disciples Withdraw from Jesus

"As a result of this many of His disciples withdrew and were not walking with Him anymore".

The phrase you mentioned, "As a result of this, many of His disciples withdrew and were not walking with Him anymore," appears to be a biblical reference. This sentence is found in the New Testament of the Bible, specifically in the Gospel of John, Chapter 6, verse 66. The verse is part of a larger narrative where Jesus speaks about being the bread of life and the importance of eating his flesh and drinking his blood metaphorically.

In this particular verse, Jesus' teachings caused controversy and were difficult for some of his followers to accept. The statement indicates that many of his disciples chose to withdraw and stop following him as a result of these teachings. It signifies a moment of disappointment or disillusionment, where individuals who had been following Jesus decided to discontinue their association with him.

Disciples' Commitment: Unwavering Trust

So Jesus said to the twelve, "You do not want to go away also, do you?" Simon Peter answered Him, "Lord, to whom shall we go? You have words of eternal life. We have believed and have come to know that You are the Holy One of God." Jesus answered them, "Did I Myself not choose you, the twelve, and yet one of you is a devil?" Now He meant Judas the son of Simon Iscariot, for he, one of the twelve, was going to betray Him.

This passage is from the New Testament of the Bible, specifically from the Gospel of John, chapter 6, verses 67-71. In this passage, Jesus is speaking to His twelve disciples, also known as the apostles, and asking if they too want to leave Him like many others who found His teachings difficult to accept.

Simon Peter, one of the apostles, responds to Jesus by affirming their commitment to Him. He acknowledges that there is nowhere else to go because Jesus has the words of eternal life. Peter expresses his belief and understanding that Jesus is the Holy One of God.

In response to Peter's declaration, Jesus mentions that although He has chosen the twelve disciples, one of them is a devil. Jesus is referring to Judas Iscariot, who would later betray Him. Jesus is aware of Judas' impending betrayal, even though the disciples are not fully aware of it at this point in the narrative.

This passage highlights the loyalty and commitment of Peter and the other disciples to Jesus, contrasting it with the impending betrayal by Judas. It also underscores Jesus' foreknowledge of events to come, including Judas' betrayal.

Deceitful Devil Among Us

The phrase "one of you is a devil" suggests that among a group of individuals, there is at least one person who is deceitful, malicious, or morally corrupt. It implies that someone within the group cannot be trusted and may be working against the interests or well-being of others. The statement can be metaphorical, indicating that someone has hidden intentions or ulterior motives, or it can be literal, suggesting that an actual evil entity or individual exists within the group. The meaning and context of this phrase may vary depending on the specific situation or conversation in which it is used.

Chapter 7

Feast of Booths Approaching

"After these things Jesus was walking in Galilee, for He was unwilling to walk in Judea because the Jews were seeking to kill Him. Now the feast of the Jews, the Feast of Booths, was near".

The passage you mentioned is from the Gospel of John in the Bible, specifically John 7:1-2. It describes a specific event in the life of Jesus. Let's break it down:

"After these things" refers to the preceding events or incidents that took place in Jesus' life, which are mentioned earlier in the Gospel of John.

"Jesus was walking in Galilee" indicates that Jesus was traveling and moving about in the region of Galilee. Galilee was a northern region of ancient Israel.

"for He was unwilling to walk in Judea because the Jews were seeking to kill Him" reveals the reason why Jesus chose to stay away from Judea, a southern region of Israel. The Jewish religious leaders and some of the people there were hostile towards Jesus and sought to kill him. Jesus avoided going there to protect himself and continue his ministry.

"Now the feast of the Jews, the Feast of Booths, was near" informs us about the approaching festival called the Feast of Booths or Tabernacles. This was one of the important Jewish festivals prescribed in the Old Testament (Leviticus 23:33-43), and it was celebrated in the fall. During this festival, Jews would live in temporary shelters or booths for seven days to commemorate the Israelites' time in the wilderness after the Exodus from Egypt.

So, this passage sets the stage for Jesus' activities and the context in which the Feast of Booths was approaching.

Skeptical Brothers Doubt

Therefore His brothers said to Him, "Leave here and go into Judea, so that Your disciples also may see Your works which You are doing. For no one does anything in secret when he himself seeks to be known publicly. If You do these things, show Yourself to the world." For not even His brothers were believing in Him.

The passage you mentioned is from the New Testament of the Bible, specifically John 7:3-5. It depicts a conversation between Jesus and his brothers. At this point in the Gospel of John, Jesus had already begun performing miracles and gaining a following of disciples.

In this particular conversation, Jesus's brothers are encouraging him to go to Judea, a region where Jerusalem is located, and perform his works openly. They suggest that if Jesus truly wants to be known publicly and gain recognition, he should not keep his actions secret but demonstrate them openly to the world. The implication is that Jesus should showcase his miracles and teachings to a larger audience to gain more followers and support.

However, the passage also highlights an important detail: "For not even His brothers were believing in Him." Despite witnessing Jesus's miracles and hearing his teachings, his own brothers did not fully believe in him as the Messiah or the Son of God at that time.

This passage provides insight into the skepticism and lack of faith that some of Jesus's closest family members had in him during his earthly ministry. It serves as a reminder that not everyone immediately recognized and accepted Jesus's divine mission, even among those who were close to him.

Timing and Testimony

"So Jesus said to them, "My time is not yet here, but your time is always opportune. The world cannot hate you, but it hates Me because I testify of it, that its deeds are evil".

This statement is attributed to Jesus in the New Testament of the Bible, specifically in the book of John, chapter 7, verses 6-7. In this passage, Jesus is speaking to his disciples and addressing the timing of his actions and the reactions he receives from the world.

When Jesus says, "My time is not yet here, but your time is always opportune," he is referring to the divine timing of his mission on Earth. He understands that there is a specific plan and purpose for his life, including his death and resurrection, and that the appropriate time for those events to occur has not yet arrived. However, he acknowledges that his disciples have the freedom to act and face opportunities as they arise in their lives.

The next statement, "The world cannot hate you, but it hates Me because I testify of it, that its deeds are evil," expresses the reason for the animosity that Jesus faces from the world. Jesus recognizes that the world, in a general sense, does not have a reason to hate his disciples because they do not challenge or confront it directly. However, Jesus, by his teachings and actions, reveals the truth about the world and exposes its sinful nature. This confrontation with the world's wrongdoing causes it to react negatively toward Jesus.

In summary, Jesus is explaining to his disciples that his actions and timing are governed by a divine plan, and while the world may not hate them, it hates him because he testifies to the world's evil deeds. This passage highlights the unique role and purpose Jesus had in confronting and challenging the prevailing norms and behaviors of his time.

Jesus' Secret Feast Attendance

Go up to the feast yourselves; I do not go up to this feast because My time has not yet fully come." Having said these things to them, He stayed in Galilee. But when His brothers had gone up to the feast, then He Himself also went up, not publicly, but as if, in secret.

The passage you mentioned is from the New Testament of the Bible, specifically from the Gospel of John, chapter 7, verses 8-10. It describes a situation involving Jesus and his brothers during a Jewish feast.

In this context, Jesus is speaking to his brothers and telling them that he will not be going up to the feast with them. He explains that his time has not yet fully come, indicating that he has a different plan or purpose that he needs to fulfill before attending the feast. As a result, he chooses to stay in Galilee while his brothers go up to the feast without him.

However, after his brothers have left for the feast, Jesus decides to go up as well. It mentions that he does so "not publicly, but as if, in secret." This suggests that Jesus does not make his presence widely known and intentionally keeps a lower profile, possibly to avoid drawing too much attention or to fulfill a particular purpose in a discreet manner.

This passage highlights Jesus' sense of timing and his adherence to a divine plan. It also emphasizes his unique role and mission, distinct from the actions and expectations of his brothers or others around him.

Seeking Jesus, Opinions, Fears

What it means, So the Jews were seeking Him at the feast and were saying, "Where is He?" There was much grumbling among the crowds concerning Him; some were saying, "He is a good man"; others were saying, "No, on the contrary, He leads the people astray." Yet no one was speaking openly of Him for fear of the Jews.

The passage you quoted appears to be from the New Testament of the Bible, specifically from the Gospel of John, chapter 7, verses 11-13. This passage describes a situation during a feast where Jews were looking for a particular person, and there were differing opinions about him among the crowds.

In the context of the Gospel of John, the person being sought is Jesus Christ. During the feast, some people recognized Jesus as a good man, while others believed that he was misleading or deceiving the people. It indicates that there was a division of opinion among the people regarding Jesus' character and teachings.

The passage also mentions that people were not openly speaking about Jesus because they feared the Jews. This likely refers to the religious authorities or leaders who held significant influence and power at the time. People may have been hesitant to express their thoughts about Jesus openly because of potential repercussions or conflicts with the established religious order.

Overall, this passage illustrates the diversity of opinions and the fear surrounding Jesus' identity and teachings during the particular feast mentioned in the Gospel of John.

Jesus teaches at feast.

"But when it was now the midst of the feast Jesus went up into the temple, and began to teach".

The statement you provided appears to be a partial quotation from the Bible, specifically from the Gospel of John, chapter 7, verse 14. Here is the complete verse for context:

"But when it was now the midst of the feast, Jesus went up into the temple and began to teach."

This verse describes an event during a feast, where Jesus went to the temple and began teaching the people. The "feast" mentioned here is likely referring to the Feast of Tabernacles (also known as the Feast of Booths), which was a significant Jewish festival.

During this festival, people would gather in Jerusalem, and it was customary for rabbis and teachers to engage in public teaching and discussions. Jesus took advantage of this opportunity and went to the temple, where he began sharing his teachings with the people who were present.

His teachings often focused on spiritual and moral matters, and he would use parables and other forms of instruction to convey his message. This particular instance of Jesus teaching in the temple during the feast highlights his role as a teacher and his desire to impart his teachings to others.

Feast, Jesus Teaches

"when it was now the midst of the feast Jesus went up into the temple".

The phrase mentioned above is from the Bible, specifically the Gospel of John, Chapter 7, Verse 14. The complete verse is as follows:

"Now about the midst of the feast Jesus went up into the temple, and taught."

This verse describes an event during a feast, likely referring to the Feast of Tabernacles, which was a significant Jewish festival. The phrase "the midst of the feast" indicates that it was during the middle or halfway point of the celebration.

In this context, "Jesus went up into the temple" means that Jesus entered the temple in Jerusalem, which was the central place of worship for the Jewish people. The temple was a significant religious and cultural site.

The phrase "and taught" indicates that Jesus began to teach or preach to the people gathered in the temple. Jesus frequently used such occasions to share his teachings, provide spiritual guidance, and engage in discussions with both his disciples and the general public.

Uneducated Man, Divine Wisdom

The Jews then were astonished, saying, "How has this man become learned, having never been educated?"

The phrase provided above is from the New Testament of the Bible, specifically in the Gospel of John, chapter 7, verse 15. In this passage, Jesus is teaching in the temple in Jerusalem during the Feast of Tabernacles. The Jews who were present were amazed at his knowledge and teaching abilities. They expressed their astonishment by saying, "How has this man become learned, having never been educated?"

The statement reflects the surprise of the Jews because Jesus, as a young man from a humble background, did not receive formal education in the prominent rabbinical schools or under well-known teachers. Yet, his teachings and wisdom were profound and deeply insightful. The Jews were puzzled as to how Jesus acquired such knowledge and spiritual understanding without the conventional educational background that would typically be associated with it.

This passage is often used to highlight Jesus' divine wisdom and his ability to teach with authority, transcending traditional educational systems. It emphasizes the extraordinary nature of Jesus' teachings and the impact they had on those who witnessed them.

Jesus' Divine Teaching Source

So Jesus answered them and said, "My teaching is not Mine, but His who sent Me. If anyone is willing to do His will, he will know of the teaching, whether it is of God or whether I speak from Myself.

This passage is from the Bible, specifically from the Gospel of John, chapter 7, verses 16-17. In this context, Jesus is speaking to a group of people who were questioning the authority and source of his teachings.

When Jesus says, "My teaching is not Mine, but His who sent Me," he is emphasizing that his teachings come from God, the one who sent him. Jesus is claiming that the authority and content of his teachings originate from a divine source.

The following verse, "If anyone is willing to do His will, he will know of the teaching, whether it is of God or whether I speak from Myself," suggests that those who are open to God's will and have a genuine desire to understand and follow it will recognize the truth in Jesus' teachings. Jesus is essentially saying that those who have a sincere and receptive heart will discern the divine nature of his message.

This passage highlights Jesus' humility and his dependence on God the Father for the authority and content of his teachings. It also emphasizes the importance of having an open and willing heart to recognize the truth and validity of his teachings as originating from God.

Seeking God's Glory

He who speaks from himself seeks his own glory; but He who is seeking the glory of the One who sent Him, He is true, and there is no unrighteousness in Him.

The phrase you mentioned appears to be a biblical verse, specifically from the New Testament of the Christian Bible. It is found in the Gospel of John, chapter 7, verse 18. Here is the verse in its context:

"He who speaks from himself seeks his own glory; but He who is seeking the glory of the One who sent Him, He is true, and there is no unrighteousness in Him." (John 7:18)

In this verse, Jesus is speaking and referring to himself. The verse highlights a distinction between those who speak on their own authority to seek personal glory and those who speak on behalf of God, seeking to glorify God rather than themselves.

The verse suggests that someone who speaks solely to promote their own interests and gain personal acclaim is not trustworthy. However, someone who speaks with the intention of honoring and bringing glory to the One who sent them (in this case, Jesus speaking of God the Father) is considered true and righteous.

This verse emphasizes the importance of humility, selflessness, and seeking to align oneself with the will and purpose of God rather than seeking personal glory or self-centered motives.

Moses' Law: Hypocrisy Exposed

Did not Moses give you the Law, and yet none of you carries out the Law? Why do you seek to kill Me?" The crowd answered, "You have a demon! Who seeks to kill You?" Jesus answered them, "I did one deed, and you all marvel. For this reason Moses has given you circumcision (not because it is from Moses, but from the fathers), and on the Sabbath you circumcise a man. If a man receives circumcision on the Sabbath so that the Law of Moses will not be broken, are you angry with Me because I made an entire man well on the Sabbath? Do not judge according to appearance, but judge with righteous judgment."

The passage you provided is from the Gospel of John in the New Testament of the Bible, specifically from John 7:19-24. Here is the passage in its entirety:

In this passage, Jesus confronts the crowd who questions His authority and accuses Him of breaking the Law of Moses. Jesus points out their inconsistency in observing the Law by referring to the practice of circumcision, which is performed on the Sabbath, a day of rest according to the Jewish law. Jesus highlights that they don't object to circumcising a man on the Sabbath to keep the Law intact, yet they criticize Him for healing a man on the Sabbath.

Jesus encourages them not to judge based on outward appearances but to exercise righteous judgment. He challenges their understanding of the Law and their hypocrisy, emphasizing that His actions align with the true spirit and purpose of the Law.

Seeking to kill Jesus

So some of the people of Jerusalem were saying, "Is this not the man whom they are seeking to kill?

The scripture you are referring to is from the New Testament of the Bible, specifically from the Gospel of John. The verse you are quoting is from John 7:25:

"So some of the people of Jerusalem were saying, 'Is this not the man whom they are seeking to kill?'"

This verse is part of a larger narrative where Jesus is teaching in the temple during the Feast of Tabernacles. There was division among the people regarding Jesus' identity and whether or not he was the Christ. Some recognized him as the one whom the religious authorities were seeking to kill, while others were uncertain about his true identity.

It is worth noting that scripture references may differ slightly depending on the translation or version of the Bible being used.

The quote provided here is from the New American Standard Bible (NASB).

Confusion about Jesus

"Look, He is speaking publicly, and they are saying nothing to Him. The rulers do not really know that this is the Christ, do they?"

The specific passage you are referring to does not match any known biblical scripture. However, I can provide you with a similar passage from the New Testament that relates to the idea of people's response to Jesus as the Christ.

In John 7:26-27, there is a discussion among the people about Jesus, and some express doubt about His identity:

"Now, look, He is speaking publicly, and they are saying nothing to Him. The rulers do not really know that this is the Christ, do they? However, we know where this man is from; but whenever the Christ may come, no one knows where He is from."

Although this passage does not exactly match your statement, it captures the essence of people's uncertainty about Jesus being the Christ and their confusion about His origins.

Jesus' Divine Mission

Then Jesus cried out in the temple, teaching and saying, "You both know Me and know where I am from; and I have not come of Myself, but He who sent Me is true, whom you do not know".

The statement you provided is a verse from the New Testament of the Bible, specifically John 7:28. In this passage, Jesus is speaking to the people in the temple during a religious festival. Let's break down the meaning of the statement:

"Then Jesus cried out in the temple, teaching and saying": This indicates that Jesus was speaking in a loud and passionate manner to get the attention of the people gathered in the temple.

"You both know Me and know where I am from": Jesus is addressing the crowd, acknowledging that they are aware of who he is and where he comes from. He is referring to his earthly identity and likely alluding to the fact that he is from the region of Galilee.

"I have not come of Myself, but He who sent Me is true": Jesus is asserting that his mission and purpose on Earth were not self-initiated or self-appointed. He claims that someone else, whom he refers to as "He who sent Me," has sent him. Jesus is indicating that his authority and teachings come from a higher power.

"Whom you do not know": Jesus adds that the people he is speaking to do not know the one who sent him, meaning they lack knowledge or recognition of God or the divine source behind Jesus' mission.

This statement highlights Jesus' belief in his divine mission and his relationship with God as the one who sent him. He is implying that the people in the temple may not fully comprehend or acknowledge the true nature of his mission and his connection to the higher power.

Scripture: I Know Him

"I know Him, because I am from Him, and He sent Me."

The quotation above is found in the New Testament of the Bible, specifically in the Gospel of John, chapter 7, verse 29 (John 7:29). In this verse, Jesus is speaking, and He says:

"But I know Him, for I am from Him, and He sent Me."

This statement by Jesus emphasizes His intimate relationship with God the Father, claiming that He knows God because He is from Him and has been sent by Him. It reflects the divine nature of Jesus as the Son of God and highlights His unique role and purpose in the world.

Seizing Jesus, Belief Spreading.

So they were seeking to seize Him; and no man laid his hand on Him, because His hour had not yet come. But many of the crowd believed in Him; and they were saying, "When the Christ comes, He will not perform more signs than those which this man has, will

He?" The Pharisees heard the crowd muttering these things about Him, and the chief priests and the Pharisees sent officers to seize Him.

The passage you provided appears to be a biblical verse from the New Testament, specifically John 7:30-32. It describes a situation where people were seeking to seize Jesus, but no one laid a hand on him because his appointed time or "hour" had not yet come.

The passage also mentions that many people in the crowd believed in Jesus because of the signs or miracles he had performed. Some among the crowd questioned whether the coming Christ (Messiah) would perform more signs than Jesus had already done.

The Pharisees, who were religious leaders, heard the murmuring and concern among the crowd about Jesus. Along with the chief priests, they sent officers or temple guards to arrest Jesus.

This passage highlights the tension and opposition that Jesus faced from certain religious authorities during his ministry. It also emphasizes the belief and admiration of many people in Jesus' miraculous abilities.

Jesus' Limited Time

Therefore Jesus said, "For a little while longer I am with you, then I go to Him who sent Me.

This statement is attributed to Jesus in the Bible, specifically in the Gospel of John (John 7:33). Jesus is speaking to a crowd of people and explaining that his time with them is limited. He says, "For a little while longer I am with you, then I go to Him who sent Me."

In this context, Jesus is referring to his impending departure from the world. He is implying that he will not be physically present with the people for much longer. The phrase "then I go to Him who sent Me" suggests that Jesus will be returning to God, whom he identifies as his sender or source.

This statement reflects Jesus' awareness of his divine mission and his forthcoming crucifixion and ascension. It indicates that his time on Earth is temporary, and he will soon be reunited with God, the one who sent him. It carries a sense of finality and points to the importance of Jesus' mission and his ultimate purpose in fulfilling God's plan.

Jews speculate Jesus' intentions.

You will seek Me, and will not find Me; and where I am, you cannot come." The Jews then said to one another, "Where does this man intend to go that we will not find Him? He is not intending to go to the Dispersion among the Greeks, and teach the Greeks, is He?

The passage you are referring to is from the New Testament of the Bible, specifically from the Gospel of John, Chapter 7, verses 33-36. In this conversation, Jesus is speaking to the Jews and making a statement about His impending departure. Let's examine the passage:

"You will seek Me, and will not find Me; and where I am, you cannot come."

The statement made by Jesus suggests that there will come a time when the Jews will try to find Him but will not be able to. Additionally, He indicates that there is a place where He will be that they cannot reach.

The Jews then speculate among themselves, wondering where Jesus intends to go that they won't be able to find Him. They consider whether He plans to go to the Dispersion among the Greeks and teach them.

The term "Dispersion" refers to the Jewish communities scattered throughout the Greek-speaking world outside of Judea. It was a common term used to refer to Jews living in the diaspora.

The Jews are questioning whether Jesus intends to leave the land of Judea and go to the Greek-speaking areas where Jewish communities existed. They find it puzzling because they believe that their knowledge of Jesus and His teachings is limited to the Jewish community, and they question if He intends to expand His teachings to the Greeks.

This passage highlights the confusion and speculation among the Jews regarding Jesus' intentions and future actions. It sets the stage for further discussions and reveals some of the misunderstandings and differing expectations surrounding Jesus' mission.

Thirst Quenched in Jesus

"Now on the last day, the great day of the feast, Jesus stood and cried out, saying, "If anyone is thirsty, let him come to Me and drink".

The sentence you provided is a quotation from the Bible, specifically John 7:37. It describes an event during the last day of a great feast, where Jesus stood up and made a proclamation. In this proclamation, Jesus said, "If anyone is thirsty, let him come to Me and drink."

This statement by Jesus is often interpreted metaphorically and symbolically. It is believed to convey a spiritual message rather than a literal call for physical thirst. In Christian theology, Jesus is often depicted as the source of spiritual fulfillment and eternal life. So, when Jesus invites anyone who is spiritually thirsty to come to Him and drink, it signifies an invitation to seek spiritual nourishment and salvation through Him.

The imagery of thirst and drinking is used metaphorically to represent the human longing for spiritual fulfillment and the need for a relationship with God. Just as physical water quenches physical thirst, Jesus is portrayed as the one who can satisfy the spiritual thirst and provide the spiritual nourishment that humans seek.

This passage is seen as an invitation to all people to come to Jesus, recognize their spiritual need, and find spiritual fulfillment through a relationship with Him.

Divisions over Jesus' Identity

He who believes in Me, as the Scripture said, 'From his innermost being will flow rivers of living water.'" But this He spoke of the Spirit, whom those who believed in Him were to receive; for the Spirit was not yet given, because Jesus was not yet glorified. Some of the people therefore, when they heard these words, were saying, "This certainly is the Prophet." Others were saying, "This is the Christ." Still others were saying, "Surely the Christ is not going to come from Galilee, is He? Has not the Scripture said that the Christ comes from the descendants of David, and from Bethlehem, the village where David was?" So a division occurred in the crowd because of Him. Some of them wanted to seize Him, but no one laid hands on Him. The officers then came to the chief priests and Pharisees, and they said to them, "Why did you not bring Him?"

The passage is from the Gospel of John in the New Testament of the Bible (John 7:37-45). It depicts a scene where Jesus is teaching in Jerusalem during the Feast of Tabernacles. Let's break down the meaning and context of the passage:

"He who believes in Me, as the Scripture said, 'From his innermost being will flow rivers of living water.'" In this statement, Jesus is referring to the belief in Him and the fulfillment of the Scriptures. He is saying that those who believe in Him will receive the Holy Spirit, represented as "rivers of living water." This suggests that through the Holy Spirit, believers will experience spiritual nourishment, renewal, and abundant life.

"But this He spoke of the Spirit, whom those who believed in Him were to receive; for the Spirit was not yet given because Jesus was not yet glorified." Here, Jesus clarifies that the "rivers of living water" represent the Holy Spirit, whom believers would receive. However, at that moment in history, the Holy Spirit had not yet been given because Jesus had not yet been glorified through His crucifixion and resurrection.

The response of the people to Jesus' teaching varied. Some considered Him to be the Prophet mentioned in the Old Testament, others believed He was the Christ (the Messiah), while some doubted whether the Christ would come from Galilee, as they believed the Scriptures indicated He would come from the descendants of David in Bethlehem. This led to division and differing opinions among the crowd regarding Jesus' identity.

The passage also mentions that some of the people wanted to seize Jesus, likely because they saw Him as a threat or were angered by His teachings. However, no one took action to apprehend Him. The officers, who were sent to arrest Jesus, did not bring Him back to the chief priests and Pharisees as instructed. This is the reason they are questioned about their failure to capture Jesus.

Overall, this passage showcases the varying beliefs and responses to Jesus' teachings and highlights the division and controversy surrounding His identity among the people of that time.

Doubtful Response to Jesus

The officers answered, "Never has a man spoken the way this man speaks." The Pharisees then answered them, "You have not also been led astray, have you? No one of the rulers or Pharisees has believed in Him, has he? But this crowd which does not know the Law is accursed." Nicodemus (he who came to Him before, being one of them) said to them, "Our Law does not judge a man unless it first hears from him and knows what he is doing, does it?" They answered him, "You are not also from Galilee, are you? Search, and see that no prophet arises out of Galilee." [Everyone went to his home.

This passage appears to be a dialogue between various individuals, including officers, Pharisees, and Nicodemus, discussing a man who speaks in a remarkable manner. Let's break it down:

"The officers answered, 'Never has a man spoken the way this man speaks.'" - The officers are remarking on the unique and powerful way this man communicates. They are expressing their astonishment at his exceptional speech.

"The Pharisees then answered them, 'You have not also been led astray, have you? No one of the rulers or Pharisees has believed in Him, has he? But this crowd which does not know the Law is accursed.'" - The Pharisees respond skeptically to the officers' statement, questioning if the officers have also been influenced or deceived by this man's words. They assert that none of the prominent leaders or Pharisees have believed in him and dismiss the crowd that follows him, considering them ignorant of the Law and cursed.

"Nicodemus (he who came to Him before, being one of them) said to them, 'Our Law does not judge a man unless it first hears from him and knows what he is doing, does it?'" - Nicodemus, a Pharisee himself, intervenes in defense of the man they are discussing. He reminds the others that according to their own law, a person should be heard and understood before passing judgment on them.

"They answered him, 'You are not also from Galilee, are you? Search, and see that no prophet arises out of Galilee.'" - The others respond to Nicodemus by questioning his origin, suggesting that he may also come from Galilee. They point out that no prophet has historically arisen from Galilee, implying that the man they are discussing cannot be significant or legitimate.

The passage concludes with the statement, "Everyone went to his home." It suggests that the conversation ends there, and each person involved departs to their respective homes.

This passage is from the New Testament in the Bible, specifically the Gospel of John (John 7:46-53). It portrays a conversation surrounding Jesus and highlights the differing opinions and skepticism of the Pharisees and other individuals regarding his teachings and identity.

Our Law and Due Process

John 7:51, is part of a larger conversation in the New Testament of the Bible. It reads as follows:

"Nicodemus, who had gone to Jesus earlier and who was one of their own number, asked, 'Does our law condemn a man without first hearing him to find out what he has been doing?'"

This verse is spoken by Nicodemus, a Pharisee and member of the Jewish ruling council, who is questioning the legality of condemning Jesus without a fair trial or due process. The phrase "our law" in this context refers to the Jewish law or the Mosaic law, which was the religious and legal system followed by the Jewish people at that time.

Nicodemus is raising a point about the importance of hearing both sides and gathering evidence before passing judgment or condemning someone. He is suggesting that it goes against their own legal principles to judge Jesus without giving him a fair opportunity to present his case.

It's worth noting that this verse is a part of a broader narrative in the Gospel of John, which focuses on the life and teachings of Jesus. The conversation in which Nicodemus raises this question takes place during a time when some people were divided in their opinions about Jesus and his identity.

Overall, John 7:51 highlights the importance of fairness, justice, and the rule of law in evaluating accusations or making judgments, even within the framework of Jewish religious and legal traditions.

Chapter 8

Teaching at the Temple

"But Jesus went to the Mount of Olives. Early in the morning He came again into the temple, and all the people were coming to Him; and He sat down and began to teach them".

The phrase you mentioned is from the New Testament of the Bible, specifically from the Gospel of John, chapter 8, verses 1-2. It describes an event where Jesus went to the Mount of Olives and then returned to the temple in Jerusalem early in the morning.

In this particular passage, it highlights Jesus' regular practice of teaching in the temple. The phrase "and all the people were coming to Him" suggests that a large crowd had gathered around Jesus, eager to listen to his teachings. Jesus then sat down, which was a common posture for teaching during that time, and began imparting his wisdom to the people.

This event serves as a testament to Jesus' popularity and his role as a teacher and spiritual leader. It also sets the stage for the events that follow in the Gospel of John, where Jesus engages in various discussions and encounters with both his followers and opponents.

Adultery Test, Jesus Responds

The scribes and the Pharisees brought a woman caught in adultery, and having set her in the center of the court, they said to Him, "Teacher, this woman has been caught in adultery, in the very act. Now in the Law Moses commanded us to stone such women; what then do You say?" They were saying this, testing Him, so that they might have grounds for accusing Him. But Jesus stooped down and with His finger wrote on the ground.

The passage above is from the New Testament of the Bible, specifically from the Gospel of John, chapter 8, verses 3-6. It recounts an incident involving Jesus and a woman who was caught in the act of adultery. Here's a breakdown of the story:

The scribes and the Pharisees were religious leaders of the time who were known for their strict adherence to the Jewish Law, particularly the laws given by Moses. They brought a woman who had been caught in the act of adultery and presented her to Jesus in the center of a courtyard.

Their intention was to test Jesus and trap Him into making a statement or taking an action that could be used against Him. According to the Law of Moses, adultery was punishable by stoning, and they wanted to see how Jesus would respond.

Instead of responding immediately, Jesus stooped down and began writing on the ground with His finger. The text does not explicitly mention what He wrote, leaving it open to interpretation and speculation.

While Jesus was writing, the religious leaders persisted in their questioning, asking Him what should be done with the woman according to the Law of Moses. They were trying to corner Him into either going against the Mosaic Law or appearing to disregard the importance of mercy and compassion.

After a moment, Jesus stood up and said, "He who is without sin among you, let him be the first to throw a stone at her." By saying this, Jesus challenged the crowd to consider their own flaws and sins before passing judgment on others. His response emphasized the importance of forgiveness, mercy, and self-reflection.

Upon hearing Jesus' words, the scribes and Pharisees were convicted by their own consciences, realizing that they themselves were not without sin. One by one, beginning with the older ones, they left the courtyard, leaving Jesus alone with the woman.

Jesus then asked the woman if anyone had condemned her. When she replied that no one had, Jesus told her, "Neither do I condemn you; go and sin no more." This statement demonstrated Jesus' compassion and forgiveness while also encouraging the woman to change her ways and live a righteous life.

This story is often interpreted as a powerful example of Jesus' teachings on mercy, forgiveness, and the importance of self-examination before judging others. It illustrates His emphasis on the spirit of the law rather than strict legalistic adherence, as well as His compassion for those who have made mistakes or sinned.

But when they persisted in asking Him, He straightened up, and said to them, "He who is without sin among you, let him be the first to throw a stone at her." Again He stooped down and wrote on the ground. When they heard it, they began to go out one by one, beginning with the older ones, and He was left alone, and the woman, where she was, in the center of the court. Straightening up, Jesus said to her, "Woman, where are they? Did no one condemn you?" She said, "No one, Lord." And Jesus said, "I do not condemn you, either. Go. From now on sin no more."]

The passage you provided is from the New Testament of the Bible, specifically from the Gospel of John, chapter 8, verses 7-11. It depicts an encounter between Jesus and a woman who was caught in the act of adultery. The religious leaders of that time brought her to Jesus, intending to trap him with a question about what should be done according to the law of Moses.

In response to their persistent questioning, Jesus straightened up and uttered the famous statement, "He who is without sin among you, let him be the first to throw a stone at her." By saying this, Jesus challenged the crowd's self-righteousness and highlighted the hypocrisy of their intentions. He suggested that only a person who is entirely free from sin has the moral authority to judge and condemn someone else.

After uttering these words, Jesus stooped down and wrote on the ground, though the specific content of what he wrote is not mentioned in the Bible. Some interpret this action as a symbolic act, representing his divine wisdom or even writing down the sins of the accusers.

The response of the religious leaders and the crowd was profound. They began to leave one by one, starting with the older individuals, and eventually, only Jesus and the accused woman remained. Jesus then asked her if anyone had condemned her, to which she replied, "No one, Lord." In response, Jesus declared, "I do not condemn you, either. Go. From now on, sin no more."

This passage is often interpreted as a display of Jesus' mercy, forgiveness, and compassion. It emphasizes the importance of recognizing one's own imperfections and refraining from harsh judgment of others. Jesus does not condone the woman's actions but offers her forgiveness and encourages her to change her ways, urging her to turn away from sin in the future.

John 8:12, Jesus: The Light of Life

Then Jesus again spoke to them, saying, "I am the Light of the world; he who follows Me will not walk in the darkness, but will have the Light of life."

The statement above is attributed to Jesus in the Christian religious tradition. In the Bible, specifically in the Gospel of John, Jesus declares, "I am the Light of the world; he who follows Me will not walk in the darkness, but will have the Light of life." This statement carries both literal and metaphorical meanings.

On a literal level, Jesus refers to himself as the "Light of the world." Light often represents illumination, clarity, and truth. In this context, Jesus is presenting himself as the source of spiritual enlightenment and guidance. The term "φῶς" (pronounced "phos") is a Greek word that translates to "light" in English. In ancient Greek philosophy, "φῶς" was often used metaphorically to represent knowledge, enlightenment, or spiritual illumination. It can also refer to physical light, as well as the concept of light in a broader sense. In various religious and philosophical contexts, "φῶς" carries symbolic significance and represents the divine or higher understanding. He claims that those who follow him will not walk in darkness, suggesting that they will be led on a path of righteousness and understanding.

Metaphorically, Jesus' statement conveys deeper spiritual truths. By identifying himself as the "Light of the world," he implies that he is the embodiment of God's truth, love, and salvation. Following Jesus means aligning oneself with his teachings, his way of life, and his example. By doing so, one can experience a transformed and meaningful life, characterized by a closer relationship with God and an understanding of divine truths.

Overall, this statement emphasizes the importance of following Jesus as a path to spiritual enlightenment, salvation, and a life filled with God's truth and love. It is a proclamation of his divine role and the transformative power of his teachings.

Jesus defends His testimony.

So the Pharisees said to Him, "You are testifying about Yourself; Your testimony is not true." Jesus answered and said to them, "Even if I testify about Myself, My testimony is true, for I know where I came from and where I am going; but you do not know where I come from or where I am going. You judge according to the flesh; I am not judging anyone. But even if I do judge, My judgment is true; for I am not alone in it, but I and the Father who sent Me. Even in your law it has been written that the testimony of two men is true. I am He who testifies about Myself, and the Father who sent Me testifies about Me." So they were saying to Him, "Where is Your Father?" Jesus answered, "You know neither Me nor My Father; if you knew Me, you would know My Father also." These words He spoke in the treasury, as He taught in the temple; and no one seized Him, because His hour had not yet come.

The passage you mentioned is from the New Testament of the Bible, specifically from the Gospel of John, chapter 8, verses 13-20. In this passage, Jesus is engaged in a discussion with the Pharisees, who were religious leaders of the time. Let's break down the meaning of the passage:

The Pharisees accuse Jesus of testifying about Himself, suggesting that His testimony is not valid or trustworthy. They are questioning the credibility of Jesus' claims. In response, Jesus defends the truthfulness of His testimony, even if it is self-proclaimed. He asserts that His knowledge of where He came from and where He is going validates the truth of His testimony.

Jesus criticizes the Pharisees for judging based on worldly standards ("according to the flesh") and declares that He does not judge anyone. However, He points out that if He were to judge, His judgment would be true because He is not alone in it; He has the Father (referring to God) who sent Him.

Jesus then refers to the principle of testimony in the Jewish law, stating that the testimony of two men is considered true. He claims that both He and the Father testify about Him, emphasizing that His testimony is not solely self-proclaimed but is supported by God's testimony.

The Pharisees further challenge Jesus by asking about His Father, implying that they are questioning His legitimacy or parentage. In response, Jesus tells them that if they knew Him, they would know His Father as well. He implies that they lack understanding and knowledge of both Himself and God.

The conversation takes place in the treasury of the temple, where Jesus is teaching. Despite the Pharisees' attempts to seize Him, they are unable to do so because His time had not yet come, indicating that it was not the appointed time for Jesus' arrest or crucifixion.

This passage reveals Jesus' confidence in His identity, His relationship with God the Father, and the validity of His testimony. It also highlights the tension and disbelief among the religious leaders of the time, as they question Jesus' authority and challenge His claims.

Jesus' Identity and Salvation

Then He said again to them, "I go away, and you will seek Me, and will die in your sin; where I am going, you cannot come." So the Jews were saying, "Surely He will not kill Himself, will He, since He says, 'Where I am going, you cannot come'?" And He was saying to them, "You are from below, I am from above; you are of this world, I am not of this world. Therefore I said to you that you will die in your sins; for unless you believe that I am He, you will die in your sins."

The passage quoted above is from the Bible, specifically from the Gospel of John, chapter 8, verses 21-24. In this passage, Jesus is speaking to a group of Jews who are questioning him and his teachings.

In the context of this passage, Jesus is referring to his impending departure from the world. He tells the people that he will go away, and they will seek him but will die in their sins. He implies that they will not be able to come to the place where he is going. This statement confuses the Jews, and they wonder if Jesus is contemplating suicide because he says, "Where I am going, you cannot come."

Jesus then explains that he is from above, meaning he is of heavenly origin, while they are from below, indicating their earthly existence. He distinguishes himself as being separate from the world. He tells them that they will die in their sins unless they believe in him as the one he claims to be.

The phrase "unless you believe that I am He" refers to the importance of recognizing Jesus' true identity. By acknowledging and believing in Jesus as the Messiah, the Son of God, they would have the opportunity to be saved from their sins. However, if they refused to believe in him, they would remain in their sins and face spiritual death.

This passage emphasizes the need for faith in Jesus as the way to eternal life and the consequence of rejecting that faith. Jesus asserts his divine nature and emphasizes the importance of recognizing and believing in him as the path to salvation.

Jesus Reveals His Identity

So they were saying to Him, "Who are You?" Jesus said to them, "What have I been saying to you from the beginning? I have many things to speak and to judge concerning you, but He who sent Me is true; and the things which I heard from Him, these I speak to the world." They did not realize that He had been speaking to them about the Father. So Jesus said, "When you lift up the Son of Man, then you will know that I am He, and I do nothing on My own initiative, but I speak these things as the Father taught Me. And He who sent Me is with Me; He has not left Me alone, for I always do the things that are pleasing to Him." As He spoke these things, many came to believe in Him.

The passage you provided is from the New Testament of the Bible, specifically from the Gospel of John, chapter 8, verses 25-30. In this passage, Jesus is engaged in a conversation with a group of people who were questioning His identity and authority.

The people asked Jesus, "Who are You?" They wanted to know who He claimed to be. In response, Jesus reminded them of what He had been teaching them from the beginning, implying that His teachings and actions should have already revealed His identity.

Jesus then stated that He had many things to speak and judge concerning them, indicating that He had much more to reveal and explain to them. He emphasized that the One who sent Him (referring to God the Father) is true and that He only speaks what He has heard from the Father.

The people did not fully understand that Jesus was speaking to them about His relationship with the Father, God. Jesus then mentioned that when they crucify Him (lift up the Son of Man), they would come to know that He is who He claims to be. He expressed that He does not act on His own initiative but speaks what the Father has taught Him. Jesus affirmed that the Father who sent Him is always with Him and has not abandoned Him, as He consistently does what pleases the Father.

As Jesus spoke these things, many people began to believe in Him. This indicates that some among the listeners were starting to grasp His true identity and message, leading to faith in Him as the Son of God.

Overall, this passage highlights Jesus' divine nature, His close relationship with God the Father, and the importance of faith and belief in Him as the sent Messiah.

True disciples find freedom.

So Jesus was saying to those Jews who had believed Him, "If you continue in My word, then you are truly disciples of Mine; and you will know the truth, and the truth will make you free." They answered Him, "We are Abraham's descendants and have never yet been enslaved to anyone; how is it that You say, 'You will become free'?" Jesus answered them, "Truly, truly, I say to you, everyone who commits sin is the slave of sin. The slave does not remain in the house forever; the son does remain forever. So if the Son makes you free, you will be free indeed. I know that you are Abraham's descendants; yet you seek to kill Me, because My word has no place in you. I speak the things which I have seen with My Father; therefore you also do the things which you heard from your father."

This passage is from the New Testament of the Bible, specifically from the Gospel of John, chapter 8, verses 31-38. It contains a dialogue between Jesus and a group of Jews who had believed in Him.

In this conversation, Jesus is addressing those Jews who had believed in Him, emphasizing the importance of continuing in His word. He tells them that if they remain committed to His teachings, they will be considered true disciples of His. Jesus then states that by following Him and His teachings, they will come to know the truth, and that truth will set them free.

The Jews respond to Jesus by expressing their confusion, stating that they are descendants of Abraham and have never been enslaved to anyone. They don't understand how Jesus is suggesting they need to be set free.

In response, Jesus explains that everyone who commits sin is actually a slave to sin. He is referring to the spiritual bondage caused by sin, which keeps people trapped and separated from God. Jesus uses the analogy of a slave not remaining in the house forever, whereas a son does. By saying this, Jesus implies that only He, as the Son of God, can grant true and everlasting freedom.

Jesus acknowledges that these Jews are descendants of Abraham, but He accuses them of seeking to kill Him because His word has no place in their hearts. He states that He speaks the things He has seen with His Father (referring to God), while they are doing the things they have learned from their earthly father (likely referring to either Abraham or the devil, depending on the context).

Overall, this passage highlights the concept of spiritual freedom through belief in Jesus and following His teachings. Jesus distinguishes between physical and spiritual slavery, asserting that true freedom comes from being released from the bondage of sin and becoming a disciple of His.

Abraham's Children Questioned

They answered and said to Him, "Abraham is our father." Jesus said to them, "If you are Abraham's children, do the deeds of Abraham. But as it is, you are seeking to kill Me, a man who has told you the truth, which I heard from God; this Abraham did not do. You are doing the deeds of your father." They said to Him, "We were not born of fornication; we have one Father: God."

The passage mentioned above is from the Bible, specifically from the New Testament, in the book of John, chapter 8, verses 39-41. In this conversation, Jesus is speaking to a group of Jews who claimed to be descendants of Abraham. Let's break down the dialogue and its meaning:

"They answered and said to Him, 'Abraham is our father.' Jesus said to them, 'If you are Abraham's children, do the deeds of Abraham.'"

The Jews are asserting their lineage and claiming Abraham as their father. Jesus challenges them by saying that being physically descended from Abraham is not enough. To truly be considered children of Abraham, they must also follow the example of Abraham's righteous actions.

"But as it is, you are seeking to kill Me, a man who has told you the truth, which I heard from God; this Abraham did not do. You are doing the deeds of your father."

Jesus points out that their actions contradict their claim of being children of Abraham. Instead of emulating Abraham's faithfulness and righteousness, they are seeking to harm Jesus, who speaks the truth that He received from God. Jesus implies that they are acting in accordance with the will of someone other than Abraham.

"They said to Him, 'We were not born of fornication; we have one Father: God.'"

The Jews respond by stating that they were not born out of wedlock and that they have God as their Father. This could be seen as a defensive response, suggesting that they are descendants of Abraham through legitimate means and that they have a special relationship with God as their Father.

This dialogue highlights the spiritual dimension of belonging to Abraham's lineage. Jesus is challenging the Jews to demonstrate the same faith and righteousness that characterized Abraham's life. He implies that their actions are more aligned with another father, possibly referring to Satan or their sinful inclinations. The Jews, in turn, claim a unique relationship with God as their Father, defending their position and denying Jesus' assertion.

The overall message conveyed is that being part of a specific lineage or making claims about one's ancestry is not enough to truly belong to a particular spiritual heritage. Actions, faith, and obedience to God's truth are what ultimately determine one's relationship with God and their inclusion in the spiritual family of Abraham.

Πορνεία: Immorality and Accusations

In John 8:41, Jesus is speaking to a group of Jews who are questioning his legitimacy and making accusations against him. The verse in question states:

"You are doing the works of your own father."

The word you mentioned, "πορνεία" (porneia), is not directly mentioned in this specific verse. However, the term "πορνεία" is a Greek word used in the New Testament and can be translated as "sexual immorality" or "fornication."

In the broader context of the Bible, sexual immorality is frequently condemned as a violation of God's commands and moral standards. It encompasses various sexual activities that deviate from God's intended design for human relationships, such as adultery, premarital sex, prostitution, and other forms of sexual misconduct.

While the term "πορνεία" may not be mentioned in John 8:41, Jesus often spoke against sexual immorality throughout his teachings, emphasizing the importance of purity and faithfulness in relationships.

Jesus' Explanation of Spiritual Allegiance

Jesus said to them, "If God were your Father, you would love Me, for I proceeded forth and have come from God, for I have not even come on My own initiative, but He sent Me. Why do you not understand what I am saying? It is because you cannot hear My word. You are of your father the devil, and you want to do the desires of your father. He was a murderer from the beginning, and does not stand in the truth because there is no truth in him. Whenever he speaks a lie, he speaks from his own nature, for he is a liar and the father of lies.

In this passage, Jesus is speaking to a group of people who do not understand his teachings and are not accepting his message. He tells them that if God were truly their Father, they would love him because he came from God and was sent by Him. Jesus emphasizes that he did not come on his own initiative, but was sent by God.

Jesus then explains why these people do not understand his words. He says that they cannot hear his word because they are not receptive to it. He identifies their spiritual allegiance by saying that they are of their father, the devil, and that they desire to do the will of their father, who is a liar and a murderer from the beginning. Jesus implies that their rejection of his message is due to their alignment with evil rather than with God.

This passage highlights the contrast between those who accept Jesus' teachings and follow God, and those who oppose him and align themselves with evil. It emphasizes the importance of love and truth in one's relationship with God and the significance of recognizing Jesus as the sent one from God.

Jesus' Truth Rejected

But because I speak the truth, you do not believe Me. Which one of you convicts Me of sin? If I speak truth, why do you not believe Me? He who is of God hears the words of God; for this reason you do not hear them, because you are not of God." The Jews answered and said to Him, "Do we not say rightly that You are a Samaritan and have a demon?" Jesus answered, "I do not have a demon; but I honor My Father, and you dishonor Me. But I do not seek My glory; there is One who seeks and judges. Truly, truly, I say to you, if anyone keeps My word he will never see death."

The passage above is from the New Testament of the Bible, specifically the Gospel of John, chapter 8, verses 45-51.

Truth vs. Unbelief

But because I speak the truth, you do not believe Me. Which one of you convicts Me of sin? If I speak truth, why do you not believe Me? He who is of God hears the words of God; for this reason you do not hear them, because you are not of God." The Jews answered and said to Him, "Do we not say rightly that You are a Samaritan and have a demon?" Jesus answered, "I do not have a demon; but I honor My Father, and you dishonor Me. But I do not seek My glory; there is One who seeks and judges. Truly, truly, I say to you, if anyone keeps My word he will never see death."

The passage you have shared is from the New Testament of the Bible, specifically from the Gospel of John, chapter 8, verses 45-51. These verses depict a conversation between Jesus and some Jews who were questioning Him.

In this dialogue, Jesus asserts that He speaks the truth and questions why the Jews do not believe Him. He challenges them to find any sin in Him and suggests that those who are truly of God would recognize and accept His words. The Jews respond by accusing Him of being a Samaritan and having a demon.

Jesus denies having a demon and states that He honors His Father, while the Jews dishonor Him. He clarifies that He does not seek personal glory but that there is One (referring to God) who seeks and judges. Jesus concludes by proclaiming that those who keep His word will never experience death.

This passage highlights the tension between Jesus and some Jewish individuals who did not accept His claims or teachings. It emphasizes the importance of faith, recognizing the truth, and following Jesus' words for eternal life.

Jews Challenge Jesus' Claim

The Jews said to Him, "Now we know that You have a demon. Abraham died, and the prophets also; and You say, 'If anyone keeps My word, he will never taste of death.'

The statement you provided appears to be a biblical reference from the New Testament of the Christian Bible, specifically from the Gospel of John, chapter 8, verse 52. In this passage, Jesus is engaged in a conversation with some Jews who were questioning his teachings and claims.

The Jews' statement reflects their disbelief and disagreement with Jesus' assertion that those who keep his word will never experience death. They accuse him of having a demon because they consider his statement to be blasphemous or absurd. They point out that both Abraham, who is revered as the founding patriarch of Judaism, and the prophets, who were esteemed figures in Jewish history, died despite their righteousness.

Essentially, the Jews are challenging Jesus' claim of offering eternal life or freedom from death to those who follow his teachings. They are expressing their skepticism and using Abraham and the prophets as examples to refute Jesus' statement.

Jesus' Authority Challenged

Surely You are not greater than our father Abraham, who died? The prophets died too; whom do You make Yourself out to be?" Jesus answered, "If I glorify Myself, My glory is nothing; it is My Father who glorifies Me, of whom you say, 'He is our God'; and you have not come to know Him, but I know Him; and if I say that I do not know Him, I will be a liar like you, but I do know Him and keep His word.

The passage you quoted is from the New Testament of the Bible, specifically from the Gospel of John, chapter 8, verses 53-55. In this conversation, the religious leaders of Jesus' time were questioning his claims and authority.

When they said, "Surely You are not greater than our father Abraham, who died? The prophets died too; whom do You make Yourself out to be?" they were questioning how Jesus could claim authority and significance greater than that of Abraham and the prophets. They were essentially asking Jesus to justify his claims and to explain who he believed himself to be.

Jesus responded by saying that if he were to glorify himself, his glory would mean nothing. Instead, he stated that it is his Father who glorifies him. In this context, Jesus was referring to God as his Father, indicating a close relationship and divine authority.

He further argued that the religious leaders did not truly know God, even though they claimed him as their God. Jesus claimed to know God intimately and to keep his word, contrasting himself with the religious leaders who were challenging him.

By saying that if he were to deny knowing God, he would be a liar like them, Jesus was emphasizing the difference between his own relationship with God and theirs. He was asserting that he truly knew and followed God, while they did not.

Overall, this passage highlights Jesus' claims of a unique relationship with God and his authority to speak on God's behalf. It is part of the broader narrative in the New Testament that portrays Jesus as the Son of God and the fulfillment of God's promises in the Old Testament.

Jesus Claims Preexistence.

Your father Abraham rejoiced to see My day, and he saw it and was glad." So the Jews said to Him, "You are not yet fifty years old, and have You seen Abraham?" Jesus said to them, "Truly, truly, I say to you, before Abraham was born, I am." Therefore they picked up stones to throw at Him, but Jesus hid Himself and went out of the temple.

The passage you mentioned is from the New Testament of the Bible, specifically from the Gospel of John, chapter 8, verses 56-59.

In this dialogue, Jesus is speaking to a group of Jews who questioned his claims about himself.

When Jesus says, "Your father Abraham rejoiced to see My day, and he saw it and was glad," he is referring to the fact that Abraham, an important figure in the Hebrew Bible, anticipated the coming of Jesus and the fulfillment of God's promises through him. Jesus is suggesting that he is the fulfillment of those promises and that Abraham, in a spiritual sense, was aware of this and rejoiced in it.

The Jews then respond by pointing out that Jesus is not even fifty years old, and they question how he could have seen Abraham who lived many centuries before. In response to their skepticism, Jesus declares, "Truly, truly, I say to you, before Abraham was born, I am."

By saying "before Abraham was born, I am," Jesus is using the present tense verb "am" to refer to himself, indicating his eternal existence. He is making a profound statement about his divine nature and claiming to be the preexistent Son of God. The phrase "I am" echoes the name of God revealed to Moses in the Old Testament when God said, "I am who I am" (Exodus 3:14).

The Jews, considering Jesus' claim to divinity as blasphemy, pick up stones to throw at him because they perceive it as a violation of their religious laws. However, Jesus manages to hide himself and leaves the temple, avoiding their attempt to harm him.

This passage illustrates the conflict between Jesus and the Jewish religious leaders of his time and highlights Jesus' claims about his identity and divine nature. It is often interpreted as a significant statement of Jesus' preexistence and his connection to the promises made to Abraham.

Chapter 9

Blind Man's Sinless Opportunity

In terms of John 9: 1 As He passed by, He saw a man blind from birth. And His disciples asked Him, "Rabbi, who sinned, this man or his parents, that he would be born blind?"

In John 9:1-2, the passage describes Jesus passing by and noticing a man who was blind from birth. His disciples, curious about the cause of the man's blindness, asked Jesus whether the man or his parents had sinned, leading to his condition.

During that time, there was a common belief among some Jewish people that physical ailments and disabilities were a direct consequence of sin. This belief was based on certain passages in the Hebrew Scriptures, such as Exodus 20:5, which states that God visits "the iniquity of the fathers on the children to the third and fourth generation." Some interpreted this to mean that the sins of the parents could be inherited by their children, resulting in physical ailments or other misfortunes.

However, Jesus provided a different perspective on the matter in John 9:3. He responded to his disciples' question by saying, "Neither this man nor his parents sinned, but this happened so that the works of God might be displayed in him." Jesus challenged the assumption that the man's blindness was a punishment for sin, asserting that it was an opportunity for God to demonstrate His power and glory through a miraculous healing.

Jesus went on to heal the blind man by spitting on the ground, making mud with the saliva, and applying it to the man's eyes. He then instructed the man to wash in the Pool of Siloam, and as the man obeyed, his sight was restored.

The story of the blind man in John 9 serves as a demonstration of Jesus' power as the light of the world, capable of bringing spiritual and physical sight to those who are in darkness. It challenges the notion of connecting physical disabilities or misfortunes with personal sin, emphasizing instead the opportunity for God's works and grace to be revealed in challenging circumstances.

Purpose in Suffering

John 9:3 is a verse from the New Testament of the Bible, specifically from the Gospel of John. In this verse, Jesus responds to a question about the cause of a man's blindness. The verse states:

"Jesus answered, 'Neither this man nor his parents sinned, but that the works of God should be revealed in him.'"

This statement by Jesus suggests that the man's blindness was not a direct result of any sin committed by him or his parents. Jesus emphasizes that the man's condition was an opportunity for God to demonstrate His power and glory through a miraculous healing. It highlights the idea that suffering and adversity can serve as a platform for God's works to be made manifest and bring about a greater purpose.

This verse raises important theological questions about the relationship between sin and suffering, as well as the role of divine intervention in human afflictions. Jesus' response challenges the notion that personal suffering is always a direct consequence of individual sins, suggesting that God's purposes can transcend human understanding.

Working while it's day.

The verse you mentioned, John 9:4, is part of a conversation between Jesus and His disciples. Here is the verse in context from the New King James Version of the Bible:

"I must work the works of Him who sent Me while it is day; the night is coming when no one can work."

In this verse, Jesus is referring to the limited time He has on Earth to accomplish the mission given to Him by God the Father. He uses the metaphor of day and night to convey the urgency of His mission and the need to act while He has the opportunity.

The phrase "We must work the works of Him who sent Me" emphasizes the importance of fulfilling God's purpose and carrying out His will. Jesus understood that His time on Earth was limited, and He needed to actively engage in the work of preaching, teaching, healing, and ultimately sacrificing Himself for the salvation of humanity.

The mention of "night is coming when no one can work" suggests that there will come a time when Jesus' earthly ministry would come to an end. This can be interpreted as referring to His impending crucifixion, death, and resurrection. After Jesus' departure, His disciples would continue the work of spreading the Gospel, but they too would face limitations and eventually reach the end of their own lives.

Overall, this verse encourages believers to be diligent and purposeful in their service to God and the work of His kingdom, making the most of the opportunities they have in this life. It serves as a reminder of the temporariness of our time on Earth and the need to prioritize and invest in what is eternally significant.

Light of the World

The verse mentioned in John 9:5, is part of a passage in the New Testament of the Bible where Jesus is speaking to his disciples and others. In this particular verse, Jesus refers to himself as "the Light of the world." Here is the full verse in context:

"As long as I am in the world, I am the light of the world." (John 9:5, NIV)

Jesus often used metaphors and symbols to explain his purpose and role to his followers. By calling himself "the Light of the world," Jesus was making a profound statement about his identity and mission. Light is commonly associated with illumination, truth, and guidance. Jesus was proclaiming that he came to bring spiritual enlightenment, truth, and salvation to the world.

In the broader context of the chapter, John 9 records the healing of a man who was born blind. After Jesus healed the man's blindness, the religious leaders questioned the man and his parents about the healing. This verse is part of Jesus' response to the situation, highlighting his divine authority and the spiritual significance of his presence in the world.

Overall, John 9:5 is a powerful declaration by Jesus, emphasizing his role as the source of spiritual light and truth in the world during his earthly ministry.

Miracle of Healing Sight

In terms of John 9:6-7 When He had said this, He spat on the ground, and made clay of the spittle, and applied the clay to his eyes, and said to him, "Go, wash in the pool of Siloam" (which is translated, Sent). So he went away and washed, and came back seeing.

John 9:6-7 describes a miracle performed by Jesus. According to the passage, Jesus spat on the ground, made clay from the spittle, and applied it to the eyes of a blind man. Then Jesus instructed the man to go and wash in the pool of Siloam. The pool of Siloam is described as "Sent" in the passage.

The blind man followed Jesus' instructions, went to the pool of Siloam, washed his eyes, and as a result, he regained his sight. The passage suggests that the blind man was healed through this act of Jesus.

This incident is significant because it demonstrates Jesus' power and ability to perform miracles. It also shows the man's faith and obedience in following Jesus' instructions, which resulted in his healing.

Identity of the Beggar

John 9:8-12 Therefore the neighbors, and those who previously saw him as a beggar, were saying, "Is not this the one who used to sit and beg?" Others were saying, "This is he," still others were saying,

"No, but he is like him." He kept saying, "I am the one." So they were saying to him, "How then were your eyes opened?" He answered, "The man who is called Jesus made clay, and anointed my eyes, and said to me, 'Go to Siloam and wash'; so I went away and washed, and I received sight." They said to him, "Where is He?" He said, "I do not know."

In this passage from the Gospel of John (John 9:8-12), the neighbors and those who had previously seen the man as a beggar are discussing his identity after his sight is miraculously restored. Some recognize him and say, "Is not this the one who used to sit and beg?" Others express uncertainty, saying, "No, but he is like him." The man himself keeps asserting, "I am the one."

Naturally, the people are curious about how the man's eyes were opened, so they ask him, "How then were your eyes opened?" He responds by recounting the events: Jesus made clay, anointed his eyes with it, and instructed him to go to the pool of Siloam and wash. The man followed Jesus' instructions, washed in the pool, and received his sight.

When the people hear the man's account, they inquire about the whereabouts of Jesus, asking him, "Where is He?" The man, however, replies, "I do not know."

This passage highlights the miraculous healing performed by Jesus, restoring the man's sight. It also illustrates the reactions of the people who knew the beggar before his transformation, their uncertainty about his identity, and their curiosity about the one who performed the healing.

Pharisees question healed man

John 9:13-15 They brought to the Pharisees the man who was formerly blind. Now it was a Sabbath on the day when Jesus made the clay and opened his eyes. Then the Pharisees also were asking him again how he received his sight. And he said to them, "He applied clay to my eyes, and I washed, and I see."

In this passage, John 9:13-15, we see the Pharisees questioning a man who had been blind but received his sight through Jesus' intervention. The event took place on the Sabbath, which was a day of rest and strict observance of religious laws for the Jewish people.

The Pharisees, who were religious leaders and experts in Jewish law, brought the man before them to investigate the circumstances of his healing. They were known for their adherence to the Sabbath laws and were concerned about any activities that they perceived as breaking those laws, including healing on the Sabbath.

The man explained to the Pharisees how Jesus had applied clay to his eyes, and after washing it off, he regained his sight. By mentioning the use of clay, the man was essentially confirming that Jesus had performed a healing act. The use of clay by Jesus in this instance could be seen as a symbolic action, representing the creative power of God in giving sight to the blind.

The Pharisees, however, were more focused on the fact that this healing took place on the Sabbath rather than the miraculous nature of the healing itself. They saw this as a violation of their strict interpretation of the Sabbath laws, which prohibited work, including healing, on that day.

This passage sets the stage for the ongoing conflict between Jesus and the Pharisees regarding his authority and the interpretation of religious laws. The Pharisees' questioning of the healed man is part of their attempts to discredit Jesus and find reasons to accuse him of wrongdoing.

Pharisees Divided on Jesus

In John 9:16, the passage describes a situation where the Pharisees were divided in their opinions about Jesus. Some of them claimed that Jesus couldn't be from God because he did not adhere to their strict interpretation of Sabbath observance. According to their understanding, Jesus performed healing miracles on the Sabbath, which they considered to be a violation of the Sabbath law.

However, there were others among the Pharisees who recognized that Jesus had the ability to perform extraordinary signs and miracles. They found it difficult to reconcile these miraculous acts with the idea that Jesus was a sinner. Therefore, they were hesitant to dismiss Jesus outright and were open to the possibility that he might be someone special.

The division among the Pharisees regarding Jesus' identity reflects the differing interpretations and beliefs held by different individuals within the group. Some were more focused on legalistic adherence to religious laws, while others were more open to evaluating Jesus based on his actions and the signs he performed.

This passage highlights the ongoing conflict and debate that surrounded Jesus during his ministry, with different groups and individuals having contrasting views on his identity and the nature of his authority.

Blind man's healing doubted.

John 17:19, So they said to the blind man again, "What do you say about Him, since He opened your eyes?" And he said, "He is a prophet." The Jews then did not believe it of him, that he had been blind and had received sight, until they called the parents of the very one who had received his sight, and questioned them, saying, "Is this your son, who you say was born blind? Then how does he now see?"

In this passage, a blind man who had been healed by Jesus is being questioned by the Jewish religious leaders. The man testifies that Jesus is a prophet because he recognizes that only a person with divine power could have healed him. However, the religious leaders are skeptical and refuse to believe that the man had been blind and received his sight. To verify his story, they call in the man's parents and question them about his condition. The leaders are trying to determine the truth of the situation and possibly disprove the miracle performed by Jesus.

This passage illustrates the skepticism and disbelief of the religious leaders despite witnessing a miraculous event. They continue to doubt the man's testimony and seek further evidence to support their disbelief.

Fearful Parents, Inquisitive Jews

John 9:20-23 His parents answered them and said, "We know that this is our son, and that he was born blind; but how he now sees, we do not know; or who opened his eyes, we do not know. Ask him; he is of age, he will speak for himself." His parents said this because they were afraid of the Jews; for the Jews had already agreed that if anyone confessed Him to be Christ, he was to be put out of the synagogue. For this reason his parents said, "He is of age; ask him."

In John 9:20-23, the parents of the man who was born blind are responding to questions from the religious leaders, the Jews, about how their son received his sight. The parents confirm that he is indeed their son and that he was born blind, but they do not know how he regained his sight or who was responsible for opening his eyes.

Their response, "Ask him; he is of age, he will speak for himself," indicates that they want the religious leaders to question their son directly about his healing. The reason for their evasive response becomes clear in the following verse, where it is explained that the parents were afraid of the Jews. The religious leaders had already made an agreement that anyone who confessed Jesus to be the Christ would be expelled from the synagogue, which was a significant social and religious consequence. Therefore, the parents chose not to provide any further information about their son's healing and directed the religious leaders to question him directly.

This passage highlights the fear and pressure faced by individuals who believed in Jesus during that time, particularly within the Jewish community. It also demonstrates the growing conflict between the religious authorities and those who recognized Jesus as the Messiah.

Blind Man's Faith

In the Gospel of John, chapter 9, verses 24-25. In this passage, the religious leaders called the man who had been blind for questioning. They wanted him to give glory to God by acknowledging that Jesus, who had healed him, was a sinner.

However, the man who had been blind responded by saying that he did not know whether Jesus was a sinner or not. He focused instead on the undeniable fact that, although he was once blind, he could now see. His response emphasizes the transformative power of Jesus' healing.

This passage reflects the man's simple yet profound testimony about the miraculous change that occurred in his life. It also highlights the contrast between the religious leaders who were skeptical of Jesus and the man who had experienced his miraculous power firsthand.

Overall, this passage reminds us that sometimes personal experiences and encounters with Jesus can be more powerful than theological debates or preconceived notions. The man's statement expresses his faith in Jesus and the evidence of his healing, even though he may not have fully understood the theological implications at that moment.

Healing Testimony Challenged.

So they said to him, "What did He do to you? How did He open your eyes?" He answered them, "I told you already and you did not listen; why do you want to hear it again? You do not want to become His disciples too, do you?"

The passage you mentioned, John 9:26-27, is part of a larger story in the Gospel of John where Jesus heals a man who was born blind. The Pharisees, who were religious leaders of the time, questioned the man about how Jesus opened his eyes.

In response to their inquiries, the man who was healed expressed his frustration with their questioning. He said, "I told you already and you did not listen; why do you want to hear it again?" Essentially, he was reminding them that he had already explained how Jesus had healed him, but they had not paid attention or accepted his testimony.

Furthermore, the man's statement, "You do not want to become His disciples too, do you?" was a challenge to the Pharisees. He questioned whether they were genuinely interested in becoming followers of Jesus. His question may have been a way to provoke them or make them reconsider their motives and intentions.

Overall, this passage highlights the skepticism and resistance of the Pharisees towards Jesus and their unwillingness to accept the man's testimony about his healing. It also emphasizes the man's frustration with their persistent questioning and his boldness in challenging their motives.

Jesus' Origin Questioned

In terms of John 9:28-33, They reviled him and said, "You are His disciple, but we are disciples of Moses. We know that God has spoken to Moses, but as for this man, we do not know where He is from." The man answered and said to them, "Well, here is an amazing thing, that you do not know where He is from, and yet He opened my eyes. We know that God does not hear sinners; but if anyone is God-fearing and does His will, He hears him. Since the beginning of time it has never been heard that anyone opened the eyes of a person born blind. If this man were not from God, He could do nothing."

In the passage you mentioned, John 9:28-33, there is a conversation taking place between the Pharisees and a man who was born blind but healed by Jesus. The Pharisees were skeptical of Jesus and questioned the legitimacy of his actions, while the man defended Jesus and expressed his belief in Him.

The Pharisees began by reviling the man and asserting their own discipleship to Moses, emphasizing their adherence to the Law of Moses. They acknowledged that God had spoken to Moses and considered themselves his disciples. However, they expressed doubt regarding Jesus, stating that they did not know where He was from.

In response, the man who was healed by Jesus pointed out the inconsistency in their arguments. He found it remarkable that the Pharisees did not know where Jesus was from, yet Jesus had opened his eyes, performing an extraordinary miracle. He stated that if Jesus were not from God, He would not have been able to perform such a miraculous act.

The man further asserted that God does not listen to sinners, but He does hear those who fear Him and do His will. The man's reasoning was that since Jesus had performed this unprecedented miracle of restoring sight to a person who was born blind, it indicated that Jesus had a special relationship with God. He concluded that Jesus must be from God because no one in history had ever opened the eyes of a person born blind.

This dialogue reflects the tension and disbelief among some religious leaders of that time regarding Jesus' identity and authority. The man who was healed saw the miraculous power of Jesus and recognized Him as being from God, while the Pharisees struggled to accept this and clung to their allegiance to Moses and the Law.

Dismissal of Blind Man

John 9:34 is a verse from the New Testament of the Bible, specifically from the Gospel of John. It recounts an incident where Jesus healed a man who was born blind. After the healing, the religious leaders of the time questioned the man about his healing and tried to discredit Jesus. The verse states:

"They answered him, 'You were born entirely in sins, and are you teaching us?' So they put him out."

In this context, the religious leaders were questioning the authority of the man who was healed, implying that his physical condition was a result of his own sins or his parents' sins. They believed that such a person had no right to teach or speak on matters of religious importance.

By saying, "You were born entirely in sins, and are you teaching us?" the religious leaders were essentially dismissing the man's ability to offer any spiritual or religious insights or teachings. They considered themselves as authoritative figures and saw the man's blindness as a sign of his inherent sinfulness.

As a result of their rejection and disbelief, they expelled the man from their presence, "So they put him out." This expulsion can be seen as an attempt to silence him and maintain their own position of power and authority.

Overall, this verse highlights the religious leaders' resistance to Jesus' teachings and their refusal to acknowledge the miraculous healing as a sign of divine intervention. It also serves as a contrast between their self-proclaimed righteousness and the humble faith of the man who was healed.

Belief in Jesus

Jesus heard that they had put him out, and finding him, He said, "Do you believe in the Son of Man?" He answered, "Who is He, Lord, that I may believe in Him?" Jesus said to him, "You have both seen Him, and He is the one who is talking with you." And he said, "Lord, I believe." And he worshiped Him.

The passage you mentioned is from the Gospel of John, specifically John 9:35-38. In this passage, Jesus has just healed a man who was blind from birth. The religious leaders were skeptical of the healing and questioned the man and his parents about it. As a result, they expelled the man from the synagogue.

Jesus then seeks out the man who was healed and asks him if he believes in the Son of Man, which is a title Jesus often used to refer to himself. The man responds by asking who the Son of Man is so that he may believe in him. Jesus identifies himself as the Son of Man, affirming that the man has seen him and that he is the one speaking to him.

Upon realizing who Jesus is, the man declares his belief by saying, "Lord, I believe," and he proceeds to worship Jesus.

This passage highlights the transformative power of encountering Jesus. The man who was once blind not only received physical healing but also came to recognize Jesus as Lord and worshiped him. It emphasizes the importance of faith and acknowledging Jesus as the Son of God.

Jesus' Purpose: Spiritual Insight

In John 9:39, Jesus is speaking metaphorically about spiritual blindness and sight. The verse can be understood in the following way:

"For judgment I came into this world": Jesus is expressing that His purpose in coming into the world is to bring about judgment or discernment. His teachings and actions bring clarity and reveal the true nature of individuals and their relationship with God.

"So that those who do not see may see": Jesus came to bring spiritual sight or understanding to those who are spiritually blind or unaware. He offers enlightenment, knowledge, and the opportunity for people to recognize and embrace the truth of God.

"And that those who see may become blind": Here, Jesus is referring to those who believe they have spiritual sight or understanding but are actually blinded by their own pride, self-righteousness, or false beliefs. He challenges their presumed knowledge and exposes their spiritual blindness.

In essence, Jesus' statement in John 9:39 emphasizes the transformative power of His teachings. He brings clarity and insight to those who are open to Him, while also challenging and humbling those who are self-assured in their own understanding. It highlights the importance of humility, openness, and the recognition of our need for spiritual guidance and enlightenment.

Pharisees' Blindness Exposed

Those of the Pharisees who were with Him heard these things and said to Him, "We are not blind too, are we?" Jesus said to them, "If you were blind, you would have no sin; but since you say, 'We see,' your sin remains.

In the verses from John 9:40-41, the Pharisees who were present with Jesus heard His teachings and asked Him a question. They said, "We are not blind too, are we?" This question can be understood as a metaphorical inquiry, rather than a literal one. The Pharisees were known for their self-righteousness and their belief that they had superior knowledge and understanding of the Scriptures.

In response to their question, Jesus said, "If you were blind, you would have no sin; but since you say, 'We see,' your sin remains." Jesus' statement here carries a spiritual meaning. He was not speaking about physical blindness but about spiritual blindness and understanding. He was pointing out that if the Pharisees acknowledged their spiritual blindness and acknowledged their need for guidance and salvation, they would be free from sin. However, because they claimed to have spiritual insight and understanding, their sin remained.

In essence, Jesus was emphasizing that humility and recognizing one's spiritual need are essential for receiving God's forgiveness and salvation. The Pharisees' self-righteousness and refusal to acknowledge their spiritual blindness hindered them from truly understanding Jesus' teachings and recognizing Him as the Messiah.

This passage serves as a warning against spiritual pride and self-assurance. It reminds us of the importance of humility, openness, and a willingness to seek God's guidance and truth rather than relying solely on our own understanding.

Chapter 10

Thief Warning: Unauthorized Access

"Truly, truly, I say to you, he who does not enter by the door into the fold of the sheep, but climbs up some other way, he is a thief and a robber.

John 10:1 is a verse from the New Testament of the Bible, specifically from the Gospel of John. In this verse, Jesus is speaking and using an analogy to describe Himself as the Good Shepherd and His followers as the sheep. Let's break down the verse and its meaning:

"Truly, truly, I say to you": Jesus often used this phrase to emphasize the importance and truthfulness of His words. It signals that what follows is a significant statement.

"He who does not enter by the door into the fold of the sheep": Jesus refers to Himself as the one who enters through the door into the fold of the sheep. The door represents the proper and legitimate way of access.

"But climbs up some other way": Here, Jesus contrasts Himself with those who try to enter the sheepfold by alternative means, not through the door. These individuals are attempting to gain access in an unauthorized and deceitful manner.

"He is a thief and a robber": Jesus categorizes those who try to enter the sheepfold in any way other than through the door as thieves and robbers. This description implies that they have malicious intentions and seek to exploit or harm the sheep.

This verse is often interpreted metaphorically to convey a spiritual truth. Jesus presents Himself as the rightful and legitimate means of access to God and salvation. He is the "door" or the only way to have a relationship with God. Those who try to approach God through any other means or teachings are considered "thieves and robbers" because they mislead people and do not offer the true path to salvation.

Overall, this verse emphasizes Jesus' role as the only true and authorized way to have a relationship with God, and it warns against false teachings or deceptive practices that may lead people astray.

Understanding John 10:2-4

But he who enters by the door is a shepherd of the sheep. To him the doorkeeper opens, and the sheep hear his voice, and he calls his own sheep by name and leads them out. When he puts forth all his own, he goes ahead of them, and the sheep follow him because they know his voice.

The passage you mentioned, John 10:2-4, is part of a metaphorical discourse in the Gospel of John where Jesus describes Himself as the Good Shepherd. In this passage, Jesus uses the analogy of a shepherd and his sheep to illustrate His relationship with His followers.

In these verses, Jesus emphasizes that the shepherd enters the sheepfold through the door, indicating that he has the rightful access and authority over the sheep. The doorkeeper recognizes the shepherd and opens the door for him, symbolizing the acceptance and recognition of Jesus' authority.

The sheep, representing the followers of Jesus, respond to the voice of the shepherd. They hear His voice and know it, indicating a close and personal relationship between the shepherd and the sheep. The shepherd knows each of his sheep by name, further highlighting the intimacy and care He has for His followers.

Furthermore, the shepherd takes the lead and goes ahead of the sheep. The sheep follow the shepherd because they recognize His voice and trust Him. This illustrates the concept of discipleship and how Jesus guides and leads His followers.

Overall, this passage portrays Jesus as the caring and authoritative Good Shepherd who knows His followers intimately, guides them, and is recognized and followed by those who belong to Him. It highlights the personal relationship between Jesus and His followers and the trust and obedience that stem from recognizing His voice.

Understanding John 10:5

"A stranger they simply will not follow, but will flee from him, because they do not know the voice of strangers."

The verse you mentioned is from the New Testament of the Bible, specifically John 10:5. In this verse, Jesus is using a metaphor to illustrate the relationship between himself (as the Good Shepherd) and his followers (as the sheep). Here is the verse in context:

"But they will never follow a stranger; in fact, they will run away from him because they do not recognize a stranger's voice." (John 10:5, NIV)

In this metaphorical context, Jesus is emphasizing that his followers, symbolized as sheep, will not listen to or follow the voice of strangers because they do not know them. The implication is that Jesus, as the Good Shepherd, has a unique and intimate relationship with his followers, and they recognize and trust his voice.

This verse is often understood to convey the idea that true followers of Jesus will discern his teachings and guidance from those of false or misleading voices. It speaks to the importance of knowing and recognizing the voice of Jesus, which comes through understanding his teachings and having a personal relationship with him.

It's important to note that the interpretation of biblical verses may vary among different individuals and religious traditions. Different scholars and readers may offer nuanced interpretations based on their understanding and context.

Understanding Jesus' Door Metaphor

This figure of speech Jesus spoke to them, but they did not understand what those things were which He had been saying to them. So Jesus said to them again, "Truly, truly, I say to you, I am the door of the sheep. All who came before Me are thieves and robbers, but the sheep did not hear them. I am the door; if anyone enters through Me, he will be saved, and will go in and out and find pasture.

In this passage from the Gospel of John, Jesus uses a figure of speech to convey a deeper spiritual truth to his listeners. Let's break down the verses you mentioned, John 10:6-9:

Verse 6: "This figure of speech Jesus spoke to them, but they did not understand what those things were which He had been saying to them."

Jesus often used parables and figurative language to teach his followers. In this instance, the people did not fully comprehend the meaning behind Jesus' words.

Verse 7: "So Jesus said to them again, 'Truly, truly, I say to you, I am the door of the sheep.'"

Jesus repeats his statement, emphasizing its importance. He declares himself as the "door" of the sheep, implying a significant role in the spiritual realm.

Verse 8: "All who came before Me are thieves and robbers, but the sheep did not hear them."

Here, Jesus contrasts himself with those who came before him, referring to false leaders or individuals who claimed to be messiahs. He portrays himself as the genuine and rightful shepherd, while others who came earlier were impostors.

Verse 9: "I am the door; if anyone enters through Me, he will be saved, and will go in and out and find pasture."

Jesus reiterates his identity as the door, emphasizing that salvation and true spiritual nourishment come through him. By entering through him, people will find salvation and experience a fulfilling and abundant life.

This passage highlights Jesus' claim to be the exclusive way to God, the only means of salvation and spiritual sustenance. Through his metaphorical depiction as the door, Jesus emphasizes the importance of accepting him and following his teachings to experience a meaningful relationship with God and eternal life.

Abundant Life Offered.

The thief comes only to steal and kill and destroy; I came that they may have life, and have it abundantly.

John 10:10 is a verse from the New Testament of the Bible, specifically from the Gospel of John. It is part of a larger passage where Jesus describes himself as the Good Shepherd who cares for his sheep. The verse states:

"The thief comes only to steal and kill and destroy; I have come that they may have life, and have it abundantly."

In this verse, Jesus contrasts himself with the thief who represents those who seek to harm and destroy. The thief symbolizes Satan or any force or entity that opposes the work of Jesus. The thief's intention is to steal, kill, and destroy, signifying the harm and negative influence that such forces can have on people's lives.

On the other hand, Jesus presents himself as the source of life and abundance. He came with the purpose of granting people a rich and fulfilling life. This abundant life encompasses spiritual, emotional, and physical well-being, and it is only made possible through a personal relationship with Jesus.

The verse highlights the stark contrast between the destructive intentions of the thief and the life-giving purpose of Jesus. It emphasizes Jesus' role as the savior and provider of abundant life for those who believe in him.

Good Shepherd's Sacrificial Love

"I am the good shepherd; the good shepherd lays down His life for the sheep.

In John 10:11, Jesus refers to Himself as the "good shepherd" and emphasizes that the good shepherd is willing to lay down his life for the sheep. This statement has deep theological significance and conveys several important teachings:

Jesus' role as the shepherd: By identifying Himself as the shepherd, Jesus is expressing His care, guidance, and protection for His followers. In biblical times, shepherds were responsible for tending and protecting their flock, ensuring their well-being and safety. Jesus, as the good shepherd, assumes this role for His followers, providing them with love, guidance, and protection.

Sacrificial love: Jesus' statement also highlights His sacrificial love for humanity. He states that the good shepherd is willing to lay down his life for the sheep. This foreshadows Jesus' ultimate act of love and sacrifice on the cross, where He willingly gave up His life to atone for the sins of humanity. Jesus' death and resurrection serve as the ultimate expression of His love and willingness to give everything for the sake of those He cares for.

Jesus' identification with His followers: The reference to sheep symbolizes believers, emphasizing their dependence on Jesus and their need for His care and leadership. As the good shepherd, Jesus identifies Himself with His followers, viewing them as His own and being deeply concerned for their well-being. The shepherd-sheep imagery underscores the intimate relationship between Jesus and His disciples, highlighting His role as their protector, provider, and guide.

Contrasting with false shepherds: In the preceding verses of John 10, Jesus criticizes the religious leaders of His time, referring to them as "thieves and robbers" who do not genuinely care for the sheep. By proclaiming Himself as the good shepherd, Jesus distinguishes Himself from these false shepherds, highlighting His genuine care, selflessness, and willingness to lay down His life for His followers. He contrasts His own sacrificial love with the self-serving motives of the religious leaders.

Overall, John 10:11 emphasizes Jesus' role as the caring and sacrificial shepherd who loves His followers to the extent of laying down His life for them. It reveals the depth of Jesus' love, His identification with His disciples, and His ultimate sacrifice on the cross for the redemption of humanity.

Shepherd vs Hired Hand

He who is a hired hand, and not a shepherd, who is not the owner of the sheep, sees the wolf coming, and leaves the sheep and flees, and the wolf snatches them and scatters them. He flees because he is a hired hand and is not concerned about the sheep.

The passage you mentioned, John 10:12-13, is part of a larger discourse by Jesus, where he uses the metaphor of a shepherd and his sheep to illustrate his role as the Good Shepherd and the relationship between him and his followers. Let's break down the meaning of these verses:

"He who is a hired hand, and not a shepherd, who is not the owner of the sheep, sees the wolf coming, and leaves the sheep and flees, and the wolf snatches them and scatters them."

In this analogy, Jesus is contrasting himself as the Good Shepherd with those who are merely hired hands. A hired hand does not have a personal stake in the sheep's well-being; they are there to fulfill a job and receive payment. When a hired hand sees a wolf coming, representing danger or a threat, their primary concern is for their own safety rather than protecting the sheep. Consequently, they abandon the sheep and run away, leaving them vulnerable to the wolf's attack. As a result, the wolf can easily snatch and scatter the sheep.

"He flees because he is a hired hand and is not concerned about the sheep."

The hired hand's action of fleeing is motivated by self-preservation rather than genuine care for the sheep. Since the hired hand lacks a personal investment in the sheep, they are not concerned about their well-being and prioritize their own safety above all else. Thus, they choose to escape the danger rather than confronting it to protect the sheep.

In contrast, Jesus presents himself as the Good Shepherd who cares deeply for his sheep. In the verses that follow (John 10:14-18), Jesus explains how he knows his sheep, they know him, and he is willing to lay down his life for them. Jesus' care for his followers goes beyond mere job responsibilities or financial gain. He is truly invested in their safety, protection, and well-being.

Overall, this passage highlights the distinction between the hired hand, who abandons the sheep in the face of danger, and the Good Shepherd, Jesus, who selflessly cares for and protects his followers, even to the point of sacrificing his own life. It emphasizes the deep love and commitment Jesus has for his disciples and the importance of having a genuine shepherd who can be trusted to lead and protect the flock.

Jesus the Good Shepherd

" I am the good shepherd, and I know My own and My own know Me, even as the Father knows Me and I know the Father; and I lay down My life for the sheep. I have other sheep, which are not of this fold; I must bring them also, and they will hear My voice; and they will become one flock with one shepherd".

John 10:14-17 is a passage from the New Testament of the Bible, specifically from the Gospel of John. In these verses, Jesus is using the metaphor of a shepherd to describe his relationship with his followers and his mission. Let's break down the key points of this passage:

"I am the good shepherd, and I know My own and My own know Me."

Jesus identifies himself as the "good shepherd." The role of a shepherd is to care for and protect the sheep, and Jesus sees himself fulfilling that role for his followers. He emphasizes the intimate relationship he has with his followers, knowing them personally, and being known by them.

"Even as the Father knows Me and I know the Father."

Here, Jesus draws a parallel between his relationship with his followers and his relationship with God the Father. He claims a deep mutual understanding and knowledge between himself and the Father, indicating the unity and closeness within the Trinity (Father, Son, and Holy Spirit).

"I lay down My life for the sheep."

Jesus speaks of his sacrificial mission. He will give up his life for the sake of his followers, symbolizing his impending crucifixion and resurrection. This act of self-sacrifice is an expression of his love and care for his followers.

"I have other sheep, which are not of this fold; I must bring them also."

Jesus indicates that his mission extends beyond his immediate followers. He speaks of "other sheep" who are not part of the current fold, referring to people who are not yet part of his immediate group of disciples. Jesus expresses his purpose to gather these individuals as well.

"They will hear My voice, and they will become one flock with one shepherd."

Jesus affirms that those who are not yet part of his fold will recognize and respond to his voice. Through this, they will become part of one unified flock, with Jesus as their shepherd. This statement conveys the idea that Jesus' mission encompasses not only his present followers but also those who will come to believe in him in the future.

Overall, this passage emphasizes Jesus' role as the good shepherd who knows and cares for his followers. It also highlights his sacrificial love and his mission to gather all people to himself, forming one unified flock under his leadership.

Jesus' authority and sacrifice.

"For this reason the Father loves Me, because I lay down My life so that I may take it again. No one has taken it away from Me, but I lay it down on My own initiative. I have authority to lay it down, and I have authority to take it up again. This commandment I received from My Father."

In the passage you mentioned, John 10:17-18, Jesus is speaking about His own authority and the purpose behind laying down His life. Let's break it down verse by verse:

"For this reason the Father loves Me because I lay down My life so that I may take it again."

Here, Jesus is stating that the Father loves Him because He willingly offers His life, and He also has the power to take it up again. This reflects Jesus' understanding of His sacrificial mission on earth, where He would offer His life as a sacrifice for the salvation of humanity.

"No one has taken it away from Me, but I lay it down on My own initiative."

Jesus emphasizes that no one is forcibly taking His life from Him. Rather, He willingly chooses to lay down His life. This demonstrates His authority and willingness to undergo the crucifixion voluntarily, fulfilling His purpose on earth.

"I have authority to lay it down, and I have authority to take it up again. This commandment I received from My Father."

Jesus asserts His authority over His own life. He has the power not only to lay down His life as a sacrifice but also to take it up again, referring to His resurrection. This authority is derived from the commandment He received from the Father, affirming the divine nature of His mission.

In these verses, Jesus is emphasizing His obedience to the Father's will and His authority over His own life. His purpose is to lay down His life as a sacrifice and then be resurrected, demonstrating His victory over death and providing salvation for all who believe in Him.

Divisions Over Jesus' Words

A division occurred again among the Jews because of these words. Many of them were saying, "He has a demon and is insane. Why do you listen to Him?" Others were saying, "These are not the sayings of one demon-possessed. A demon cannot open the eyes of the blind, can he?"

In John 10:19-21, the passage describes a division among the Jews due to Jesus' words. Some people accused Jesus of having a demon and being insane, questioning why others would listen to Him. However, there were others who held a different view and argued that Jesus' words couldn't be those of a demon-possessed individual. They reasoned that a demon would not be able to perform miracles such as opening the eyes of the blind.

This passage reflects the differing opinions and reactions of the people who encountered Jesus during His ministry. Some were skeptical and hostile, attributing His actions and teachings to demonic influence and mental instability. Others, however, recognized the power and wisdom in His words and deeds, acknowledging that they were not the result of demonic possession.

Throughout the Gospels, we see similar instances where people had varying responses to Jesus' teachings and miracles. These divisions among the Jews were indicative of the controversy and disagreement surrounding Jesus' identity and mission. Some accepted Him as the Messiah, while others rejected Him.

It is important to note that the interpretations and reactions of the people mentioned in this passage are specific to the historical context and the individuals involved. The passage provides insight into the diverse reactions that Jesus elicited, but it does not determine the truth of Jesus' claims or his actual mental state.

Feast of Dedication Walk

At that time the Feast of the Dedication took place at Jerusalem; it was winter, and Jesus was walking in the temple in the portico of Solomon.

John 10:22-23 is a passage from the New Testament of the Bible that describes an event during the Feast of the Dedication in Jerusalem, where Jesus was walking in the temple in the portico of Solomon. Here is the passage for reference:

"Then came the Festival of Dedication at Jerusalem. It was winter, and Jesus was in the temple courts walking in Solomon's Colonnade." (John 10:22-23, NIV)

The Feast of the Dedication, also known as Hanukkah or the Festival of Lights, is not mentioned in the Old Testament because it occurred after the completion of the Hebrew Bible. It commemorates the rededication of the Second Temple in Jerusalem after its desecration by the forces of Antiochus IV Epiphanes, a Greek ruler, in the 2nd century BCE. The events of Hanukkah are described in the books of Maccabees, which are not part of the Hebrew Bible but are included in the Catholic and Eastern Orthodox Christian canons.

According to the passage, it was winter and Jesus was walking in the temple in the portico of Solomon. The portico of Solomon was a covered walkway or colonnade on the east side of the temple courtyard. It was a place where people would gather and walk, and it provided shelter from the elements. The passage does not provide further details about the specific purpose or action taking place during Jesus' presence in the temple at that time.

Overall, this passage serves as a historical reference, mentioning the time of year and Jesus' location during the Feast of the Dedication in Jerusalem.

Unbelieving Jews question Jesus

The Jews then gathered around Him, and were saying to Him, "How long will You keep us in suspense? If You are the Christ, tell us plainly." Jesus answered them, "I told you, and you do not believe; the works that I do in My Father's name, these testify of Me. But you do not believe because you are not of My sheep. My sheep hear My voice, and I know them, and they follow Me; and I give eternal life to them, and they will never perish; and no one will snatch them out of My hand. My Father, who has given them to Me, is greater than all; and no one is able to snatch them out of the Father's hand. I and the Father are one."

In John 10:24-30, a group of Jews gathered around Jesus and questioned Him, asking how long He would keep them in suspense and whether He was the Christ, or the Messiah. Jesus responded by saying that He had already told them, but they did not believe Him. He pointed to the works He had done in His Father's name as evidence of His identity.

Jesus then explained that their unbelief was due to the fact that they were not His sheep. He used the metaphor of sheep and a shepherd to illustrate His relationship with His followers. He said that His sheep hear His voice, and He knows them, and they follow Him. He emphasized that He gives eternal life to His sheep, and they will never perish, nor will anyone be able to snatch them out of His hand.

Furthermore, Jesus affirmed that His Father, who had given the sheep to Him, was greater than all, and no one could snatch them out of the Father's hand. Jesus concluded by stating, "I and the Father are one," indicating His unity with God the Father.

This passage highlights the relationship between Jesus and His followers, emphasizing the belief in Him as the Christ, the reception of eternal life through Him, and the assurance of security and protection in His care. It also presents Jesus' claim of unity with God the Father, affirming His divinity.

Stoning over blasphemy

The Jews picked up stones again to stone Him. Jesus answered them, "I showed you many good works from the Father; for which of them are you stoning Me?" The Jews answered Him, "For a good work we do not stone You, but for blasphemy; and because You, being a man, make Yourself out to be God."

In the passage you mentioned, John 10:31-33, the Jews were preparing to stone Jesus. He responded by asking them why they were planning to stone Him despite the good works He had shown them from the Father. The Jews then explained that they wanted to stone Him not because of His good works, but because they believed He was committing blasphemy. They accused Him of claiming to be God while being a mere man.

This interaction between Jesus and the Jews highlights a recurring theme in the Gospel of John, where Jesus often faces opposition and criticism from religious leaders who do not believe in His divinity. The Jews saw His claims as blasphemous because they believed in the oneness and uniqueness of God.

In the following verses, Jesus defends His claims and explains His relationship with the Father, emphasizing His unity with God and His divine nature. This discourse leads to a further confrontation between Jesus and the Jews regarding His identity and His authority.

Overall, this passage underscores the conflict between Jesus and the religious establishment of His time, as well as the significance of Jesus' claims about His relationship with God.

Blasphemy Defense: Works & Scriptures

In terms of John 10:34-38 Jesus answered them, "Has it not been written in your Law, 'I said, you are gods'? If he called them gods, to whom the word of God came (and the Scripture cannot be broken), do you say of Him, whom the Father sanctified and sent into the world, 'You are blaspheming,' because I said, 'I am the Son of God'? If I do not do the works of My Father, do not believe Me; but if I do them, though you do not believe Me, believe the works, so that you may know and understand that the Father is in Me, and I in the Father."

In John 10:34-38, Jesus is responding to the Jews who accuse Him of blasphemy for claiming to be the Son of God. Let's break down the passage and understand its meaning.

Jesus begins by referring to a passage in the Jewish Law, specifically Psalm 82:6, where it says, "I said, 'You are gods.'" Jesus uses this reference to make a point. If God Himself called certain individuals "gods" in the Scriptures, how can they accuse Him of blasphemy for calling Himself the Son of God?

Jesus emphasizes that if those to whom the word of God came were called "gods," it is even more appropriate for Him, whom the Father sanctified and sent into the world, to claim to be the Son of God. He suggests that the Jews' accusation of blasphemy against Him is unfounded.

Moreover, Jesus points out that if His works do not align with the works of the Father, then the Jews have a reason not to believe Him. He challenges them to examine His works, which demonstrate His alignment with the Father's will. By performing these works, Jesus invites them to know and understand that the Father is in Him and He is in the Father.

In summary, Jesus uses this passage to defend His claim as the Son of God, arguing that if even humans were called "gods" in Scripture, His claim is not blasphemous. He encourages the Jews to look at His works as evidence of His divine mission and His unity with the Father.

Belief in Jesus Grows

Therefore they were seeking again to seize Him, and He eluded their grasp. And He went away again beyond the Jordan to the place where John was first baptizing, and He was staying there. Many came to Him and were saying, "While John performed no sign, yet everything John said about this man was true." Many believed in Him there.

The passage is from the Gospel of John, specifically John 10:39-42. In these verses, it is mentioned that some people were attempting to seize Jesus, but he managed to evade their grasp. Afterward, Jesus went back to the place where John the Baptist had first been baptizing beyond the Jordan River, and he stayed there.

At that location, many people came to Jesus and acknowledged that although John the Baptist hadn't performed any miracles or signs, everything he had said about Jesus was true. As a result, many individuals believed in Jesus at that place.

This passage highlights the recognition and acceptance of Jesus as the Messiah based on the testimony of John the Baptist. It also emphasizes the significance of faith and belief in Jesus, even without witnessing miraculous signs or wonders.

Chapter 11

Mary's Anointing & Lazarus

"Now a certain man was sick, Lazarus of Bethany, the village of Mary and her sister Martha. It was the Mary who anointed the Lord with ointment, and wiped His feet with her hair, whose brother Lazarus was sick".

In the passage of John 11:1-2, it provides some background information about a man named Lazarus who was sick. It identifies Lazarus as being from Bethany, the village where Mary and her sister Martha also lived. The passage also mentions Mary's act of anointing the Lord with ointment and wiping His feet with her hair.

This particular event of Mary anointing Jesus and wiping His feet with her hair is recorded in a different passage in the New Testament, specifically in John 12:1-8. In that account, Mary anoints Jesus' feet with expensive perfume, and Judas Iscariot, one of Jesus' disciples, objects to the perceived waste of the valuable ointment.

It's important to note that the passage in John 11:1-2 doesn't provide detailed information about the act of anointing. Instead, it simply identifies Mary as the one who performed the anointing mentioned in John 12. The purpose of mentioning this in John 11:2 may be to establish the identity of Mary and her relationship to Lazarus, who was sick and later raised from the dead by Jesus in the subsequent verses.

Delay for Lazarus

So the sisters sent word to Him, saying, "Lord, behold, he whom You love is sick." But when Jesus heard this, He said, "This sickness is not to end in death, but for the glory of God, so that the Son of God may be glorified by it." Now Jesus loved Martha and her sister and Lazarus. So when He heard that he was sick, He then stayed two days longer in the place where He was.

In John 12:3-6, the passage describes a situation where the sisters, Mary and Martha, send word to Jesus about their brother Lazarus being sick. They inform Jesus, whom they refer to as "Lord," that the one whom Jesus loves is ill. Upon hearing this, Jesus responds by saying that Lazarus' sickness is not meant to end in death but for the glory of God. Jesus states that through Lazarus' illness, the Son of God will be glorified.

It is mentioned in the passage that Jesus loved Martha, her sister Mary, and Lazarus. Despite hearing about Lazarus' sickness, Jesus intentionally stays where He is for two more days before going to see him.

This passage sets the stage for the subsequent events in John 11, where Jesus ultimately raises Lazarus from the dead. By delaying His arrival and allowing Lazarus to die, Jesus demonstrates His power over death and brings glory to God through the miraculous resurrection. This event is one of the significant signs or miracles recorded in the Gospel of John that testify to Jesus' identity as the Son of God.

Disciples' Concerns: Going Again?

Then after this He said to the disciples, "Let us go to Judea again." The disciples said to Him, "Rabbi, the Jews were just now seeking to stone You, and are You going there again?"

In the passage you mentioned, John 11:7-8, Jesus tells his disciples, "Let us go to Judea again." The disciples express their concern to Jesus, saying, "Rabbi, the Jews were just now seeking to stone You, and are You going there again?"

This conversation takes place in the context of the events leading up to the resurrection of Lazarus. Jesus had received news that Lazarus, whom He loved, was seriously ill in Bethany, which was near Jerusalem in Judea. However, the disciples were apprehensive about returning to Judea because of the hostility Jesus had previously faced there.

Earlier in the Gospel of John, there were instances where Jewish religious leaders and others had attempted to arrest or stone Jesus due to his teachings and claims of divinity. So, the disciples were concerned for Jesus' safety and questioned His decision to go back to Judea, where the opposition was strong.

However, Jesus had a divine purpose in mind. He knew that Lazarus had died and that His presence was needed for a significant miracle—the raising of Lazarus from the dead. Jesus reassured his disciples and explained the importance of their journey, expressing that this event would bring glory to God and strengthen the faith of those who witnessed it.

Ultimately, Jesus' decision to return to Judea and perform the miraculous resurrection of Lazarus was part of God's plan to reveal His power, demonstrate His authority over life and death, and foreshadow His own resurrection. It also served as a pivotal event that intensified the opposition against Jesus, leading to his eventual arrest, crucifixion, and resurrection.

This passage highlights the disciples' concern for Jesus' safety and their difficulty in understanding the full scope of God's plan. It also showcases Jesus' unwavering determination to fulfill His mission, even in the face of danger and opposition.

Jesus: Light in Darkness

Jesus answered, "Are there not twelve hours in the day? If anyone walks in the day, he does not stumble, because he sees the light of this world. But if anyone walks in the night, he stumbles, because the light is not in him."

In the passage of John 11:9-10, Jesus is using a metaphorical language to explain a spiritual concept. Let's take a closer look at the verses:

"Jesus answered, 'Are there not twelve hours in the day? If anyone walks in the day, he does not stumble, because he sees the light of this world. But if anyone walks in the night, he stumbles, because the light is not in him.'"

In this statement, Jesus is using the concept of daylight and nighttime to convey a deeper meaning about spiritual understanding and guidance. The "day" represents the time when Jesus was physically present in the world, while the "night" represents a time of spiritual darkness or ignorance.

Jesus is essentially saying that if someone walks in the day, meaning they follow Him and His teachings, they will not stumble or go astray because they have the light of the world, which is the truth and guidance provided by Jesus Himself. The light represents knowledge, understanding, and the path to salvation.

On the other hand, if someone walks in the night, meaning they reject or ignore Jesus and His teachings, they will stumble and face difficulties because they lack the spiritual light. Without the light of Christ, they are more susceptible to making wrong decisions and being led astray.

Overall, this passage emphasizes the importance of following Jesus, who is the light of the world. By walking in His light, we gain spiritual insight and direction, which helps us navigate life's challenges and avoid stumbling.

Jesus' metaphorical explanation.

This He said, and after that He said to them, "Our friend Lazarus has fallen asleep; but I go, so that I may awaken him out of sleep." The disciples then said to Him, "Lord, if he has fallen asleep, he will recover." Now Jesus had spoken of his death, but they thought that He was speaking of literal sleep. So Jesus then said to them plainly, "Lazarus is dead, and I am glad for your sakes that I was not there, so that you may believe; but let us go to him."

In the passage of John 11:11-15, Jesus is speaking to his disciples about Lazarus, who had died. Let's break down the passage and its meaning:

"This He said, and after that He said to them, 'Our friend Lazarus has fallen asleep; but I go, so that I may awaken him out of sleep.'" - Jesus uses the metaphor of sleep to refer to Lazarus' death. He implies that Lazarus' death is temporary and compares it to a sleep from which he will awaken him.

"The disciples then said to Him, 'Lord, if he has fallen asleep, he will recover.'" - The disciples misunderstand Jesus' metaphor and think that Lazarus is simply asleep and will naturally recover. They do not realize that Jesus is referring to Lazarus' death.

"Now Jesus had spoken of his death, but they thought that He was speaking of literal sleep." - The passage clarifies that Jesus had actually been talking about Lazarus' death, but the disciples misunderstood and thought he was speaking about ordinary sleep.

"So Jesus then said to them plainly, 'Lazarus is dead, and I am glad for your sakes that I was not there, so that you may believe; but let us go to him.'" - Jesus corrects the disciples' misunderstanding and plainly states that Lazarus has died. He explains that he is glad he was not there when Lazarus died so that the disciples can witness the power of his resurrection and come to believe in him more strongly. Jesus then tells them that they should go to Lazarus.

This passage highlights Jesus' ability to bring the dead back to life and his desire to strengthen the faith of his disciples through this miracle. By using the metaphor of sleep, Jesus foreshadows Lazarus' resurrection, emphasizing that death is not the end but a temporary state that can be reversed by his power.

Thomas' commitment to follow.

Therefore Thomas, who is called Didymus, said to his fellow disciples, "Let us also go, so that we may die with Him."

John 11:16 is a verse from the New Testament of the Bible, specifically from the Gospel of John. In this verse, Thomas, also known as Didymus, makes a statement to his fellow disciples regarding their intentions to go with Jesus to a place where He had previously encountered opposition and danger.

The context of this verse is the story of the resurrection of Lazarus. Jesus received news that Lazarus, a close friend, was very sick. However, instead of immediately going to heal Lazarus, Jesus waited for a few days. When Jesus finally decided to go to Judea, where Lazarus lived, the disciples expressed concern for His safety. They reminded Jesus that the people in that area had recently tried to stone Him.

It is in this context that Thomas speaks up and encourages the other disciples to join Jesus on the journey, even if it means facing danger and potentially death. Thomas's statement, "Let us also go, so that we may die with Him," can be seen as an expression of loyalty and commitment. Despite the risks involved, Thomas is willing to follow Jesus to the point of death if necessary.

This verse highlights Thomas's willingness to stand with Jesus, even in the face of adversity. It also reflects the disciples' growing understanding that Jesus' mission would ultimately lead to His death. Thomas's words reveal his determination to remain faithful to Jesus, even if it meant sharing in His suffering and possibly losing his own life.

It's important to note that this verse emphasizes Thomas's doubts and struggles, as he was often known as "Doubting Thomas" due to his initial skepticism regarding Jesus' resurrection. However, this statement showcases a different side of Thomas's character, demonstrating his willingness to accompany Jesus on a perilous journey despite his doubts.

Jesus Raises Lazarus.

"So when Jesus came, He found that he had already been in the tomb four days. Now Bethany was near Jerusalem, about two miles off; and many of the Jews had come to Martha and Mary, to console them concerning their brother".

John 11:17-19 is a passage from the New Testament of the Bible that describes an event involving Jesus, Martha, Mary, and their deceased brother Lazarus. Here's the passage:

"So when Jesus came, He found that he had already been in the tomb four days. Now Bethany was near Jerusalem, about two miles off; and many of the Jews had come to Martha and Mary, to console them concerning their brother."

This passage sets the stage for the miracle that Jesus performs in raising Lazarus from the dead. When Jesus arrives in Bethany, he discovers that Lazarus had already been dead for four days and had been buried in a tomb. Bethany was a village close to Jerusalem, located about two miles away. Martha and Mary, the sisters of Lazarus, had many Jews from the surrounding area come to their house to offer them condolences and support during their time of mourning.

This passage serves as the backdrop for the miraculous event that follows, where Jesus demonstrates his power over death by raising Lazarus back to life.

Martha's Faith in Resurrection

Martha therefore, when she heard that Jesus was coming, went to meet Him, but Mary stayed at the house. Martha then said to Jesus, "Lord, if You had been here, my brother would not have died. Even now I know that whatever You ask of God, God will give You." Jesus said to her, "Your brother will rise again." Martha said to Him, "I know that he will rise again in the resurrection on the last day."

In the passage from John 11:20-24, Martha, the sister of Lazarus, goes to meet Jesus upon hearing that He is coming. Mary, another sister of Lazarus, stays at the house. When Martha meets Jesus, she expresses her faith and lament, saying that if Jesus had been there earlier, her brother would not have died. She also acknowledges her belief that whatever Jesus asks of God, God will grant Him.

In response, Jesus tells Martha that her brother will rise again. Martha, understanding the Jewish belief in the resurrection, affirms her faith in the future resurrection on the last day. She expresses her knowledge and expectation that her brother will experience resurrection at the end of time.

This conversation sets the stage for one of the most significant miracles performed by Jesus. Later in the story, Jesus raises Lazarus from the dead, demonstrating His power over death and foreshadowing His own resurrection. The passage highlights Martha's faith in Jesus and her belief in the future resurrection, while also pointing to Jesus as the source of life and resurrection.

Resurrection and Eternal Life

Jesus said to her, "I am the resurrection and the life; he who believes in Me will live even if he dies, and everyone who lives and believes in Me will never die. Do you believe this?" She said to Him, "Yes, Lord; I have believed that You are the Christ, the Son of God, even He who comes into the world."

In John 11:25-27, Jesus has a conversation with Martha, the sister of Lazarus, who had died. Jesus declares, "I am the resurrection and the life; he who believes in Me will live even if he dies, and everyone who lives and believes in Me will never die." He then asks Martha if she believes this statement.

Martha responds to Jesus by saying, "Yes, Lord; I have believed that You are the Christ, the Son of God, even He who comes into the world." Her response affirms her faith in Jesus as the Messiah, the Son of God.

This passage highlights the central message of Jesus' ministry, which is that through faith in Him, believers can have eternal life. Jesus presents Himself as the source of resurrection and life, promising that those who believe in Him will live even if they physically die. Moreover, He assures Martha that everyone who lives and believes in Him will never experience spiritual death.

Martha's response demonstrates her conviction that Jesus is the Christ, the promised Messiah, and the Son of God who came into the world. Her affirmation reveals her faith and recognition of Jesus' divine identity.

The dialogue between Jesus and Martha emphasizes the core Christian belief in the power of Jesus as the giver of eternal life and the importance of faith in Him for salvation.

Mary Responds to Jesus

When she had said this, she went away and called Mary her sister, saying secretly, "The Teacher is here and is calling for you." And when she heard it, she got up quickly and was coming to Him.

The passage you mentioned is from the Gospel of John, specifically John 11:28-29. It describes a scene where a woman, possibly Martha, goes to Mary, her sister, after speaking with Jesus. She tells Mary secretly that the Teacher (referring to Jesus) is present and is asking for her. Mary responds by quickly getting up and going to Jesus.

This passage is part of the larger story of the resurrection of Lazarus. In the preceding verses, Lazarus, who was a close friend of Jesus, had died. Jesus arrived in Bethany, where Lazarus and his sisters Martha and Mary lived, and Martha went out to meet him. They had a conversation about faith and Jesus being the resurrection and the life.

After their conversation, Martha went to Mary and informed her that Jesus was asking for her. Mary, upon hearing this, immediately went to Jesus. This episode demonstrates Mary's eagerness to be in the presence of Jesus and her response to his call.

This passage highlights the personal relationship and trust that Martha, Mary, and Lazarus had with Jesus. It also emphasizes their faith in him as the Teacher and their willingness to follow his instructions.

Mary's Grief and Faith

Now Jesus had not yet come into the village, but was still in the place where Martha met Him. Then the Jews who were with her in the house, and consoling her, when they saw that Mary got up quickly and went out, they followed her, supposing that she was going to the tomb to weep there. Therefore, when Mary came where Jesus was, she saw Him, and fell at His feet, saying to Him, "Lord, if You had been here, my brother would not have died."

In this passage from John 11:30-32, we witness a significant moment in the story of Jesus and Lazarus. Let's break it down:

"Now Jesus had not yet come into the village, but was still in the place where Martha met Him."

At the beginning of the passage, Jesus had not yet entered the village where Lazarus lived. He remained in the place where He had met Martha, Lazarus's sister, earlier.

"Then the Jews who were with her in the house, and consoling her, when they saw that Mary got up quickly and went out, they followed her, supposing that she was going to the tomb to weep there."

The scene shifts to a house where Jews had gathered to console Martha and Mary over the death of Lazarus. When Mary suddenly gets up and leaves the house, the Jews assume that she is going to the tomb to mourn there. Consequently, they follow her.

"Therefore, when Mary came where Jesus was, she saw Him, and fell at His feet, saying to Him, 'Lord, if You had been here, my brother would not have died.'"

Mary arrives at the place where Jesus is, and upon seeing Him, she falls at His feet in a posture of reverence. Overwhelmed with grief, Mary expresses her profound faith in Jesus, stating that if He had been present earlier, her brother Lazarus would not have died.

This passage sets the stage for the pivotal event of Lazarus's resurrection, which occurs shortly after. It showcases the depth of

Mary's trust in Jesus and her conviction that He has the power to perform miracles, even in the face of death.

Jesus' Compassionate Response

When Jesus therefore saw her weeping, and the Jews who came with her also weeping, He was deeply moved in spirit and was troubled, and said, "Where have you laid him?" They said to Him, "Lord, come and see." Jesus wept. So the Jews were saying, "See how He loved him!" But some of them said, "Could not this man, who opened the eyes of the blind man, have kept this man also from dying?"

In the passage you mentioned, John 11:33-37, we witness a poignant moment in the life of Jesus. He arrives at the tomb of his dear friend Lazarus, who had passed away. The sight of Lazarus' sister, Mary, weeping, as well as the Jews who accompanied her, deeply affects Jesus. He is moved in his spirit and troubled by the sorrow around him.

Jesus asks, "Where have you laid him?" and the people respond by inviting him to come and see. At this point, Jesus weeps. His tears are a profound expression of his compassion and empathy for those who are mourning. The Jews who witness Jesus' tears remark, "See how He loved him!" They are moved by the visible display of Jesus' deep affection for Lazarus.

However, there are also some who question why Jesus, who had performed miracles such as opening the eyes of the blind man, did not prevent Lazarus from dying. Their skepticism stems from a lack of understanding and a limited perspective on Jesus' purpose and mission.

This passage showcases Jesus' humanity, as he experiences and shares in the pain and sorrow of those around him. It also reveals his divine love and the depth of his compassion for humanity. Jesus' subsequent actions in raising Lazarus from the dead further exemplify his power over death and his ability to bring about resurrection and new life.

Resurrection of Lazarus

So Jesus, again being deeply moved within, came to the tomb. Now it was a cave, and a stone was lying against it. Jesus said, "Remove the stone." Martha, the sister of the deceased, said to Him, "Lord, by this time there will be a stench, for he has been dead four days." Jesus said to her, "Did I not say to you that if you believe, you will see the glory of God?"

In the Bible passage you mentioned, John 11:38-40, the story revolves around the resurrection of Lazarus, who had been dead for four days. Let's break down the verses and their meaning:

Verse 38: "So Jesus, again being deeply moved within, came to the tomb. Now it was a cave, and a stone was lying against it."

This verse sets the scene where Jesus arrives at the tomb of Lazarus. It emphasizes that Jesus was deeply moved within, possibly expressing his compassion and empathy for the situation.

Verse 39: "Jesus said, 'Remove the stone.' Martha, the sister of the deceased, said to Him, 'Lord, by this time there will be a stench, for he has been dead four days.'"

Jesus instructs the people present to remove the stone that was blocking the entrance to the tomb. However, Martha, Lazarus' sister, expresses concern about the stench that would arise from the decaying body since Lazarus had been dead for four days. Her statement reflects the belief at the time that after three days, decay and decomposition would have set in, leading to an unpleasant odor.

Verse 40: "Jesus said to her, 'Did I not say to you that if you believe, you will see the glory of God?'"

In response to Martha's concern, Jesus reassures her that if she believes, she will witness the glory of God. He is reminding her of his earlier statements about the power of faith and the ability of God to perform miracles. Jesus is about to demonstrate God's power by raising Lazarus from the dead.

These verses highlight Jesus' authority and power over death. Despite the physical limitations and the cultural understanding of death, Jesus is about to perform a miraculous act, demonstrating his divine nature and the power of belief in God.

Jesus' Gratitude and Miraculous Confirmation

In terms of John 11:41-42 So they removed the stone. Then Jesus raised His eyes, and said, "Father, I thank You that You have heard Me. I knew that You always hear Me; but because of the people standing around I said it, so that they may believe that You sent Me."

In John 11:41-42, we find the account of Jesus performing a miracle, specifically raising Lazarus from the dead. Let's break down the passage and its significance:

"So they removed the stone." This refers to the tomb where Lazarus had been buried. Jesus, along with the people present, ordered the stone covering the entrance to be removed.

"Then Jesus raised His eyes and said, 'Father, I thank You that You have heard Me.'" Before performing the miracle, Jesus directed His attention to the heavens and expressed gratitude to God the Father. He acknowledged that God had already heard Him.

"I knew that You always hear Me; but because of the people standing around I said it, so that they may believe that You sent Me." Jesus affirmed His confidence that God always hears Him. However, He verbalized His prayer aloud for the sake of the people witnessing the event. By openly praying to God, Jesus intended to strengthen the faith of those present, so that they would believe that God had sent Him.

This passage emphasizes Jesus' close relationship with the Father and His desire to demonstrate His divinity to the people. By performing this miraculous act, Jesus sought to bolster the faith of those witnessing it and confirm that He was indeed sent by God.

Raise Lazarus, disbelief reported.

When He had said these things, He cried out with a loud voice, "Lazarus, come forth." The man who had died came forth, bound hand and foot with wrappings, and his face was wrapped around with a cloth. Jesus said to them, "Unbind him, and let him go." Therefore many of the Jews who came to Mary, and saw what He had done, believed in Him. But some of them went to the Pharisees and told them the things which Jesus had done.

The passage you're referring to is from the New Testament of the Bible, specifically John 11:43-46. It describes the miraculous event where Jesus raises Lazarus from the dead. Here's a breakdown of the events:

Jesus had been conversing with Martha, the sister of Lazarus, and comforting her about her brother's death.

Standing before the tomb where Lazarus was buried, Jesus cried out with a loud voice, saying, "Lazarus, come forth!"

Miraculously, Lazarus, who had been dead for four days, emerged from the tomb. He was still wrapped in burial clothes, with his face covered by a cloth.

Jesus commanded those around him to unbind Lazarus and let him go, freeing him from the burial wrappings.

As a result of witnessing this incredible miracle, many of the Jews who had come to console Mary, Lazarus's sister, believed in Jesus. They saw the power of God at work through Him and recognized Him as the Messiah.

However, there were also some individuals who witnessed this event and were not convinced. They went to the Pharisees, who were religious leaders and opponents of Jesus, and reported what they had seen.

This passage highlights Jesus' divine power over life and death, foreshadowing His own resurrection that would take place later. It also reveals the different reactions people had to this miracle, with some believing and others opposing Jesus by informing the Pharisees.

Concerns over Jesus' Influence

Therefore the chief priests and the Pharisees convened a council, and were saying, "What are we doing? For this man is performing many signs. If we let Him go on like this, all men will believe in Him, and the Romans will come and take away both our place and our nation."

In the passage you mentioned from John 11:47-48, the chief priests and the Pharisees are expressing their concern about Jesus and the signs, or miracles, that He is performing. They are worried about the growing popularity of Jesus and the impact it may have on their own positions and the political situation with the Romans.

The chief priests and the Pharisees were part of the religious and political leadership in Jerusalem. They saw Jesus as a threat to their authority and influence over the Jewish people. They were also concerned about the Romans' response to Jesus' growing popularity.

The phrase "If we let Him go on like this, all men will believe in Him" suggests that they were aware of the impact Jesus' teachings and miracles were having on the people. They feared that more and more people would follow Jesus, which could potentially lead to a rebellion against Roman rule. They were worried that such a rebellion would not only result in the loss of their own positions and authority but also lead to reprisals from the Romans, who were occupying Judea at that time.

The mention of "both our place and our nation" refers to their concern that the Romans would view Jesus' popularity as a threat to their political stability and respond by taking away their power and potentially even dismantling the nation of Israel. They were worried about the consequences that Jesus' actions and teachings might have for their own status and the fragile political situation with the Romans.

These verses demonstrate the growing conflict and tension between Jesus and the religious and political authorities of His time, who saw Him as a threat to their power and feared the consequences of His teachings and miracles.

Caiaphas Prophecy and Plot.

But one of them, Caiaphas, who was high priest that year, said to them, "You know nothing at all, nor do you take into account that it is expedient for you that one man die for the people, and that the whole nation not perish." Now he did not say this on his own initiative, but being high priest that year, he prophesied that Jesus was going to die for the nation, and not for the nation only, but in order that He might also gather together into one the children of God who are scattered abroad. So from that day on they planned together to kill Him.

The passage is from the Gospel of John, specifically John 11:49-53. In this passage, Caiaphas, who was the high priest at that time, makes a statement regarding the fate of Jesus.

Caiaphas, speaking to the other religious leaders, expresses the belief that it would be better for one man, Jesus, to die for the people rather than the entire nation perishing. John's Gospel adds a comment that Caiaphas made this statement not on his own initiative but rather as a prophetic utterance. The text suggests that, being the high priest, Caiaphas unknowingly prophesied that Jesus would die for the nation, and not only for the nation but also to bring together the scattered children of God.

The passage goes on to state that, following Caiaphas' statement, the religious leaders began to plan together to kill Jesus. This sets the stage for the events leading to Jesus' crucifixion.

The significance of this passage is that it highlights the role of Jesus' death in God's plan for salvation. It suggests that Jesus' sacrificial death would serve a larger purpose, beyond just the nation of Israel, by gathering together the scattered children of God, referring to believers from different backgrounds.

It's important to note that interpretations of biblical passages may vary among different individuals and Christian denominations. The interpretation provided here offers a general understanding of the passage, but there may be additional layers of meaning and theological perspectives that could be explored.

Jesus Withdraws to Ephraim

Therefore Jesus no longer continued to walk publicly among the Jews, but went away from there to the country near the wilderness, into a city called Ephraim; and there He stayed with the disciples.

In the verse of John 11:54, it states that Jesus no longer walked publicly among the Jews and went away to the country near the wilderness, specifically to a city called Ephraim. It also mentions that He stayed there with His disciples.

This verse is significant because it shows a shift in Jesus' public ministry and His approach to dealing with the growing opposition from religious leaders and others who sought to harm Him. Jesus had been performing miracles and teaching publicly in various regions, but as His popularity grew and the opposition intensified, He chose to withdraw to a less populated area.

Ephraim was a small city located about 12 miles northeast of Jerusalem, and it provided a relatively secluded location for Jesus and His disciples to retreat to. This move allowed Jesus to continue teaching and preparing His disciples without attracting unnecessary attention or interference from those who opposed Him.

By withdrawing from public view, Jesus could also focus more on teaching and mentoring His disciples in a more intimate setting. He could provide them with additional instruction, answer their questions, and prepare them for the challenges they would face in the future. This period of seclusion in Ephraim served as a time of concentrated teaching and preparation for both Jesus and His disciples.

It's important to note that the specific events and timeline during this period are not extensively detailed in the Gospel accounts. The Gospel of John, in particular, focuses more on Jesus' teachings and interactions during His public ministry rather than providing a comprehensive chronology of events.

Passover Pilgrimage to Jerusalem

Now the Passover of the Jews was near, and many went up to Jerusalem out of the country before the Passover to purify themselves.

John 11:55 is a verse from the New Testament of the Bible, specifically the Gospel of John. It states: "Now the Passover of the Jews was near, and many went up to Jerusalem out of the country before the Passover to purify themselves." This verse serves as a historical and contextual statement, highlighting the timing and purpose of people's journeys to Jerusalem before the Passover.

During the time of Jesus, the Passover was a significant Jewish festival commemorating the liberation of the Israelites from slavery in Egypt. It was one of the three major pilgrimage festivals in ancient Israel, alongside the Feast of Unleavened Bread and the Feast of Weeks (Pentecost).

According to Jewish law, people were required to be ritually pure in order to participate fully in the Passover observance. Ritual purity involved various practices such as ceremonial cleansing and abstaining from certain impurities. Those who were living outside of Jerusalem would make a pilgrimage to the city in order to purify themselves before the Passover.

Therefore, John 11:55 indicates that many Jews from different parts of the country traveled to Jerusalem before the Passover to undergo the necessary purification rituals, ensuring their readiness to participate in the festival.

Seeking Jesus' Whereabouts

So they were seeking for Jesus, and were saying to one another as they stood in the temple, "What do you think; that He will not come to the feast at all?" Now the chief priests and the Pharisees had given orders that if anyone knew where He was, he was to report it, so that they might seize Him.

The passage you mentioned is from the Gospel of John, specifically John 11:56-57. In these verses, it describes a situation where people were looking for Jesus and discussing whether he would attend a feast.

According to the passage, the people were gathered in the temple and questioning whether Jesus would come to the feast at all. This indicates that Jesus' whereabouts were uncertain at that time, and there was speculation among the people about whether he would make an appearance.

The passage also mentions that the chief priests and the Pharisees had given orders for anyone who knew where Jesus was to report it. Their intention was to seize Jesus. This shows that the religious leaders were actively seeking to apprehend Jesus, likely due to the growing influence and popularity he had gained.

This passage sets the stage for the events that follow, leading to Jesus' arrest and subsequent crucifixion. The religious authorities were determined to stop Jesus, and their plans eventually culminated in his arrest, trial, and crucifixion.

Chapter 12

Anointing and objection

The passage of John 11:1-8, actually describes the events leading up to the anointing of Jesus by Mary in Bethany. The anointing itself is described in a later chapter, John 12:1-8. Let's take a closer look at the events and the significance of this event.

In John 11:1-8, it is mentioned that Jesus came to Bethany, where Lazarus, whom Jesus had raised from the dead, was residing. Jesus was invited to a supper in Bethany, hosted by Martha, and Lazarus was also present. This event occurred six days before the Passover.

In John 12:1-8, we find the account of Mary's act of anointing Jesus with a pound of very costly perfume of pure nard. She poured the perfume on Jesus' feet and wiped them with her hair, causing the fragrance to fill the house. Judas Iscariot, one of Jesus' disciples, objected to this act, suggesting that the perfume could have been sold for a high price and the money given to the poor. However, the text explains that Judas was not genuinely concerned about the poor but had ulterior motives. He was a thief and would often steal from the money box.

Jesus responded to Judas' objection, saying, "Let her alone so that she may keep it for the day of My burial. For you always have the poor with you, but you do not always have Me." Jesus acknowledged the importance of caring for the poor but also recognized the significance of this moment and Mary's act of anointing Him.

The anointing of Jesus by Mary with the expensive perfume carries symbolic meaning. In biblical times, anointing was often associated with acts of consecration, honor, and preparation for burial. By anointing Jesus with the costly perfume, Mary demonstrated her deep love and devotion to Him, acknowledging His impending death and burial.

Jesus, in turn, defended Mary's action, appreciating her act of worship and recognizing its significance. He acknowledged that while caring for the poor is important, this particular act of anointing held special meaning and should not be hindered.

This event also foreshadowed Jesus' upcoming crucifixion and burial. It highlighted the contrast between Mary's act of selfless devotion and Judas' selfish motives, leading to his later betrayal of Jesus.

Overall, this passage emphasizes the love, devotion, and sacrifice expressed through Mary's act of anointing Jesus, while also shedding light on the character of Judas and the approaching events leading to Jesus' crucifixion.

Threat to Lazarus

The large crowd of the Jews then learned that He was there; and they came, not for Jesus' sake only, but that they might also see Lazarus, whom He raised from the dead. But the chief priests planned to put Lazarus to death also; because on account of him many of the Jews were going away and were believing in Jesus.

In the passage of John 12:9-11, a significant event takes place involving Jesus, Lazarus, and the crowd of Jews. Here's a breakdown of what happens:

The large crowd of Jews learns that Jesus is present: Word spreads among the people that Jesus is in a particular location. This news attracts a crowd of Jews who are curious to see Him.

The crowd's interest in Lazarus: The crowd's curiosity extends beyond Jesus Himself. They also want to see Lazarus, a man whom Jesus had recently raised from the dead. Lazarus's resurrection had created quite a stir, and people were eager to witness this miraculous event for themselves.

The chief priests' sinister plan: However, not everyone is pleased with Lazarus's resurrection and the impact it is having. The chief priests, who were religious leaders with authority, see Lazarus as a threat. They perceive that Lazarus's presence and his resurrection are causing many Jews to believe in Jesus. This challenges their own influence and power.

The plot to kill Lazarus: As a result of their fear and concern, the chief priests devise a plan to put Lazarus to death. By eliminating Lazarus, they hope to quell the growing belief in Jesus among the Jews. They view Lazarus as a pivotal figure whose continued existence poses a risk to their authority.

In this passage, we see the contrasting reactions of the crowd and the chief priests to Lazarus's resurrection. While the crowd is fascinated and drawn to Jesus because of this miracle, the chief priests view it as a threat to their religious authority and conspire to eliminate Lazarus.

Triumphal Entry: Jesus Welcomed

On the next day the large crowd who had come to the feast, when they heard that Jesus was coming to Jerusalem, took the branches of the palm trees and went out to meet Him, and began to shout, "Hosanna! Blessed is He who comes in the name of the Lord, even the King of Israel."

The passage you mentioned is from the Gospel of John, specifically John 12:12-13. This event is often referred to as the Triumphal Entry or Palm Sunday, and it describes the scene when Jesus arrived in Jerusalem a few days before his crucifixion.

According to the passage, a large crowd had gathered in Jerusalem for the feast (likely the Passover), and when they heard that Jesus was coming, they went out to meet him. They took branches from palm trees and waved them in the air as a sign of honor and celebration. The people also shouted, "Hosanna! Blessed is He who comes in the name of the Lord, even the King of Israel."

The phrase "Hosanna" is an exclamation of praise or joy, often used in religious contexts. In this context, it expresses the crowd's recognition of Jesus as the long-awaited Messiah, the one who comes in the name of the Lord. By proclaiming him as the King of Israel, they acknowledged Jesus as the fulfillment of the Messianic prophecies from the Hebrew Scriptures.

This event is significant in the Christian tradition as it marks the beginning of Jesus' final week before his crucifixion and resurrection. The waving of palm branches and the joyful shouts of the crowd symbolize the people's anticipation and hope for Jesus as the Messiah and King. The account of the Triumphal Entry is found in all four Gospels, highlighting its importance in the life and ministry of Jesus.

Understanding Jesus' Triumphal Entry

Jesus, finding a young donkey, sat on it; as it is written, "Fear not, daughter of Zion; behold, your King is coming, seated on a donkey's colt." These things His disciples did not understand at the first; but when Jesus was glorified, then they remembered that these things were written of Him, and that they had done these things to Him.

The passage above is from the New Testament of the Bible, specifically the Gospel of John, chapter 12, verses 14-16. In these verses, it is described how Jesus found a young donkey and sat on it. This act is connected to a prophecy found in the Old Testament, specifically in Zechariah 9:9, which says, "Rejoice greatly, Daughter Zion! Shout, Daughter Jerusalem! See, your king comes to you, righteous and victorious, lowly and riding on a donkey, on a colt, the foal of a donkey."

At the time when Jesus entered Jerusalem riding on a donkey, His disciples did not fully understand the significance of this event or its connection to the prophecy. However, after Jesus was glorified, which refers to His crucifixion, resurrection, and ascension, the disciples remembered the prophecy and understood that these things were written about Jesus and that they had actively participated in fulfilling them.

This event is often referred to as the Triumphal Entry or Palm Sunday, and it holds significant symbolic meaning. The act of Jesus riding into Jerusalem on a donkey was seen as a fulfillment of messianic prophecies and was also a humble declaration of His kingship. The people in Jerusalem greeted Him with palm branches and praised Him as the King who comes in the name of the Lord.

This passage underscores the fulfillment of prophecy and the gradual understanding and revelation of Jesus' identity by His disciples. It highlights the importance of recognizing and interpreting the Scriptures in light of the life, ministry, and ultimate sacrifice of Jesus Christ.

Pharisees Concerned About Jesus

So the people, who were with Him when He called Lazarus out of the tomb and raised him from the dead, continued to testify about Him. For this reason also the people went and met Him, because they heard that He had performed this sign. So the Pharisees said to one another, "You see that you are not doing any good; look, the world has gone after Him."

In John 12:17-19 of the Bible, it describes a scene where the people who witnessed Jesus calling Lazarus out of the tomb and raising him from the dead continued to testify about Him. News of this miraculous event spread, and as a result, people were drawn to meet Jesus. The Pharisees, who were religious leaders and often in opposition to Jesus, observed the growing popularity and remarked to one another, "You see that you are not doing any good; look, the world has gone after Him."

This passage highlights the impact of Jesus' miraculous works on the people and the divided responses they generated. The resurrection of Lazarus was a powerful sign of Jesus' authority and divinity, and it attracted significant attention and curiosity from the crowds. Some people were convinced by these signs and began to follow Jesus, recognizing Him as the Messiah. However, the Pharisees, who were threatened by Jesus' popularity and his teachings that challenged their authority, viewed the situation with concern and frustration.

This passage serves as a turning point in the Gospel of John, as the events surrounding Lazarus' resurrection and the subsequent reactions set the stage for the escalating conflict between Jesus and the religious leaders, leading to His eventual arrest and crucifixion.

Greeks at the Feast

"Now there were some Greeks among those who were going up to worship at the feast".

John 12:20 is a verse from the New Testament in the Bible. In this verse, it is mentioned that there were some Greeks among the people who were going up to worship at the feast.

This verse is part of the larger context of Jesus' ministry and the events leading up to his crucifixion. The feast mentioned here is likely the Passover feast, which was a significant Jewish festival held in Jerusalem. Many Jews from various places would travel to Jerusalem to participate in the feast and offer sacrifices at the temple.

The mention of Greeks in this context suggests that there were non-Jews, specifically Greeks, who were interested in the Jewish faith and wanted to participate in the worship practices during the feast. It indicates that the message and influence of Jesus were spreading beyond the Jewish community and attracting attention from people of different backgrounds.

This verse also serves as a precursor to the following events in the Gospel of John, where Jesus talks about his impending death and the significance of his sacrifice for all people, not just the Jewish nation. It highlights the universal nature of Jesus' mission and the potential inclusion of Gentiles (non-Jews) in the message of salvation.

Desire to See Jesus

These then came to Philip, who was from Bethsaida of Galilee, and began to ask him, saying, "Sir, we wish to see Jesus." Philip came and told Andrew; Andrew and Philip came and told Jesus. And Jesus answered them, saying, "The hour has come for the Son of Man to be glorified.

In John 12:21-23, a group of people approached Philip, who was from Bethsaida in Galilee, expressing their desire to see Jesus. Philip then consulted with Andrew, and together they informed Jesus about the request. In response, Jesus declared that the time had arrived for the Son of Man (referring to himself) to be glorified.

This passage marks a significant point in the Gospel of John, as it signifies a turning point in Jesus' ministry. The request to see Jesus and Jesus' subsequent statement about his glorification foreshadows the events that would unfold leading up to his crucifixion and resurrection. The hour mentioned by Jesus refers to the impending culmination of his earthly mission and the fulfillment of God's plan for salvation.

Death and Eternal Life

Truly, truly, I say to you, unless a grain of wheat falls into the earth and dies, it remains alone; but if it dies, it bears much fruit. He who loves his life loses it, and he who hates his life in this world will keep it to life eternal.

John 12:24-25 is a passage from the New Testament of the Bible, specifically from the Gospel of John. It is part of a larger conversation where Jesus is teaching his disciples and others about various aspects of his ministry and the nature of following him.

Let's break down the passage and explore its meaning:

"Truly, truly, I say to you, unless a grain of wheat falls into the earth and dies, it remains alone; but if it dies, it bears much fruit."

In this verse, Jesus uses a metaphor of a grain of wheat to illustrate a spiritual principle. He compares his own impending death and resurrection to a grain of wheat that must fall into the earth and die in order to produce a bountiful harvest. Jesus is foreshadowing his crucifixion and subsequent resurrection, where his death would bring forth salvation and new life for all who believe in him. Just as a grain of wheat must be buried in the ground and die to fulfill its purpose of producing many more grains, Jesus had to die to accomplish his mission of redemption.

"He who loves his life loses it, and he who hates his life in this world will keep it to life eternal."

In the following verse, Jesus speaks about the paradoxical nature of true discipleship. He emphasizes that those who cling too tightly to their earthly life and prioritize their own self-preservation will ultimately lose it. However, those who are willing to let go of their worldly desires and priorities, even to the point of "hating" their life in this world, will find eternal life.

This teaching challenges individuals to reevaluate their values and priorities. It calls for a willingness to sacrifice one's own self-centered desires and ambitions for the sake of following Jesus and living in accordance with God's kingdom principles. By letting go of selfish pursuits and aligning their lives with God's purposes, believers can experience true and abundant life that extends beyond the temporal boundaries of this world.

Overall, these verses convey important spiritual truths about the nature of Jesus' mission, the call to self-sacrifice, and the promise of eternal life for those who follow him wholeheartedly.

Serve, Follow, Be Honored

John 12:26 is a verse from the Bible that states: "If anyone serves Me, he must follow Me; and where I am, there My servant will be also. If anyone serves Me, the Father will honor him." This verse is attributed to Jesus, who was speaking to His disciples and a crowd of people.

In this verse, Jesus is conveying the importance of discipleship and following Him. He emphasizes that those who serve Him must also be willing to follow Him. This means not only accepting His teachings but also modeling their lives after His example.

Jesus also promises that where He is, His servant will be there as well. This statement implies a close and intimate relationship between Jesus and His followers. It suggests that by serving and following Jesus, individuals will have a personal connection with Him and will be united with Him in purpose and mission.

Furthermore, Jesus assures that if anyone serves Him, the Father will honor that person. This speaks of the recognition and approval that God the Father bestows upon those who serve Jesus faithfully. It indicates that God acknowledges and rewards the service rendered to His Son.

Overall, John 12:26 encourages believers to not only profess their faith in Jesus but also to actively serve Him and follow His teachings. It emphasizes the close relationship between Jesus and His disciples and highlights the divine honor and approval that comes from serving Him.

Jesus Troubled, Father Glorified

"Now My soul has become troubled; and what shall I say, 'Father, save Me from this hour'? But for this purpose I came to this hour. Father, glorify Your name." Then a voice came out of heaven: "I have both glorified it, and will glorify it again." So the crowd of people who stood by and heard it were saying that it had thundered; others were saying, "An angel has spoken to Him." Jesus answered and said, "This voice has not come for My sake, but for your sakes.

In John 12:27-30, Jesus expresses that His soul has become troubled. He contemplates what He should say to the Father, whether to ask to be saved from the hour that is approaching. However, Jesus acknowledges that He came to this hour for a purpose. He then prays to the Father, saying, "Father, glorify Your name."

In response to Jesus' prayer, a voice comes from heaven, affirming that the Father has already glorified His name and will do so again. The people who were present at that moment heard the voice but did not fully understand its significance. Some thought it was thunder, while others believed that an angel had spoken to Jesus.

Jesus responds to the crowd, explaining that the voice from heaven was not for His sake but for their sake. It was a confirmation of God's presence and His affirmation of Jesus' mission. The voice was intended to provide assurance and strengthen the faith of those who heard it.

Overall, this passage highlights Jesus' obedience to the Father's will, even in the face of trouble and uncertainty. It also underscores the importance of God's glorification and the purpose behind Jesus' impending hour, which refers to His upcoming crucifixion and resurrection.

Crucifixion and Universal Salvation

John 12:31-34 Now judgment is upon this world; now the ruler of this world will be cast out. And I, if I am lifted up from the earth, will draw all men to Myself." But He was saying this to indicate the kind of death by which He was to die.

The passage you mentioned is from the New Testament of the Bible, specifically John 12:31-34. In this passage, Jesus is speaking about the impending judgment upon the world and the casting out of the ruler of this world, which is commonly interpreted to refer to Satan or the forces of evil. Jesus then goes on to say that if He is "lifted up from the earth," He will draw all people to Himself. The phrase "lifted up from the earth" is understood to refer to Jesus' crucifixion, and His statement is seen as an indication of the manner in which He would die.

This passage carries multiple layers of meaning. Firstly, it points to the impending judgment upon the world and the defeat of the ruler of this world through Jesus' sacrificial death on the cross. It signifies the overthrowing of the forces of evil and the establishment of God's kingdom. Secondly, it emphasizes the redemptive nature of Jesus' death, suggesting that His crucifixion would serve as a means of drawing all people to Himself. It signifies the universal scope of salvation offered through Jesus' sacrifice, as people from all walks of life are called to be reconciled with God through Him.

Overall, this passage from John's Gospel highlights the impending judgment, the defeat of evil, and the redemptive significance of Jesus' death on the cross as a means of drawing all people to Himself.

Confused Crowd Questions Identity

The crowd then answered Him, "We have heard out of the Law that the Christ is to remain forever; and how can You say, 'The Son of Man must be lifted up'? Who is this Son of Man?"

In John 12:34, the crowd responds to Jesus' statement about being lifted up by asking, "We have heard out of the Law that the Christ is to remain forever; and how can You say, 'The Son of Man must be lifted up'? Who is this Son of Man?

The phrase "Son of Man" is a title that Jesus often used to refer to himself throughout the Gospels. It is a Messianic title with roots in the Old Testament book of Daniel (Daniel 7:13-14), where the prophet Daniel has a vision of "one like a son of man" who is given authority and an everlasting kingdom by God.

By referring to himself as the Son of Man, Jesus is affirming his identity as the long-awaited Messiah and the fulfillment of Old Testament prophecies. However, the crowd seems to be confused by Jesus' statement about being lifted up. They express their understanding that the Christ (or Messiah) is supposed to remain forever, and they question how Jesus can claim to be the Son of Man who must be lifted up.

The concept of Jesus being "lifted up" refers to his crucifixion, where he would be raised up on a cross. Jesus is foreshadowing his impending death and the purpose behind it, which is to provide salvation for humanity through his sacrificial atonement. The crowd's confusion may stem from their expectation of a triumphant and everlasting Messiah, rather than one who would suffer and die.

The crowd's question, "Who is this Son of Man?" reflects their lack of understanding or perhaps their desire for further clarification regarding Jesus' identity and mission.

Light's Importance & Spiritual Transformation

In terms of John 12:35-36, So Jesus said to them, "For a little while longer the Light is among you. Walk while you have the Light, so that darkness will not overtake you; he who walks in the darkness does not know where he goes. While you have the Light, believe in the Light, so that you may become sons of Light."

In John 12:35-36, Jesus is addressing a crowd and making a metaphorical reference to himself as the "Light." Let's break down the verses and explore their meaning:

"So Jesus said to them, 'For a little while longer the Light is among you. Walk while you have the Light, so that darkness will not overtake you; he who walks in the darkness does not know where he goes.'"

In this statement, Jesus is acknowledging that his presence, represented as the Light, is with the people for a limited time. He is implying that he will not be physically present with them indefinitely. By urging them to "walk while you have the Light," he encourages them to make the most of his presence and teachings while they still have the opportunity. Walking in the Light refers to following his teachings and guidance.

Jesus also warns about the darkness overtaking those who do not walk in the Light. The darkness here represents ignorance, spiritual blindness, or separation from God. By choosing to walk in the darkness, a person lacks spiritual understanding and direction, not knowing where they are going. It suggests that without following the teachings of Jesus, individuals may find themselves lost and without a clear path in life.

"While you have the Light, believe in the Light, so that you may become sons of Light."

In this part of the passage, Jesus emphasizes the importance of believing in the Light, which refers to believing in him and his teachings. By accepting Jesus as the Light and following his teachings, individuals can become "sons of Light," indicating a spiritual transformation or adoption into a new way of life characterized by spiritual enlightenment and divine connection.

Overall, this passage highlights the temporary nature of Jesus' physical presence, the importance of following his teachings, and the transformative power of believing in him as the Light. It encourages individuals to seek spiritual understanding, guidance, and transformation through a relationship with Jesus.

Unbelief despite signs

These things Jesus spoke, and He went away and hid Himself from them. But though He had performed so many signs before them, yet they were not believing in Him. This was to fulfill the word of Isaiah the prophet which he spoke: "Lord, who has believed our report? And to whom has the arm of the Lord been revealed?" For this reason they could not believe, for Isaiah said again, "He has blinded their eyes and He hardened their heart, so that they would not see with their eyes and perceive with their heart, and be converted and I heal them." These things Isaiah said because he saw His glory, and he spoke of Him.

In John 12:36-41, Jesus speaks and then goes away and hides Himself from the people. Despite having performed many signs before them, they still did not believe in Him. This is seen as the fulfillment of the prophecy spoken by Isaiah, where he asks who has believed their report and to whom has the arm of the Lord been revealed.

The reason why they could not believe, according to Isaiah, is that God had blinded their eyes and hardened their hearts so that they would not see with their eyes, perceive with their hearts, be converted, and receive healing. Isaiah spoke these words because he saw the glory of Jesus and prophesied about Him.

This passage highlights the unbelief of the people despite witnessing Jesus' signs and miracles. It also emphasizes the fulfillment of the prophecies spoken by Isaiah regarding the response of the people to Jesus' ministry. The hardening of their hearts and blindness to the truth are presented as part of God's plan and fulfillment of prophecy.

Fearful rulers and Jesus' mission

Nevertheless many even of the rulers believed in Him, but because of the Pharisees they were not confessing Him, for fear that they would be put out of the synagogue; for they loved the approval of men rather than the approval of God. And Jesus cried out and said, "He who believes in Me, does not believe in Me but in Him who sent Me. He who sees Me sees the One who sent Me. I have come as Light into the world, so that everyone who believes in Me will not remain in darkness. If anyone hears My sayings and does not keep them, I do not judge him; for I did not come to judge the world, but to save the world.

In the passage of John 12:42-47, the context is a discussion of belief in Jesus and the fear of openly confessing Him. It mentions that many rulers believed in Jesus, but they were afraid to confess their faith because of the Pharisees. The rulers were concerned about being expelled from the synagogue, and they valued the approval of men more than the approval of God.

In response to this situation, Jesus cried out and made several statements. He said that those who believe in Him are actually believing in the One who sent Him, referring to God the Father. Jesus emphasized the unity between Himself and the Father, stating that seeing Him is equivalent to seeing the Father.

Jesus also proclaimed that He came as a Light into the world, offering salvation and delivering people from darkness. He emphasized that those who believe in Him will not remain in darkness but will have the light of life.

Furthermore, Jesus clarified that He did not come to judge the world but to save it. He explained that those who hear His teachings and do not keep them are not judged by Him because His purpose was not to condemn but to bring salvation.

In summary, this passage highlights the conflict between the rulers' belief in Jesus and their fear of openly confessing Him. Jesus emphasizes the unity between Himself and the Father, stating that belief in Him is belief in God. He also emphasizes that He came to bring light and salvation to the world, and His mission was not to judge but to save.

Rejecting Jesus, Final Judgment

He who rejects Me and does not receive My sayings, has one who judges him; the word I spoke is what will judge him at the last day. For I did not speak on My own initiative, but the Father Himself who sent Me has given Me a commandment as to what to say and what to speak. I know that His commandment is eternal life; therefore the things I speak, I speak just as the Father has told Me."

The passage you mentioned, John 12:48-50, is from the New Testament of the Bible and is part of Jesus' teachings. In these verses, Jesus emphasizes the importance of accepting Him and His teachings, stating that those who reject Him and do not receive His sayings will be judged. He explains that the words He speaks will serve as the basis for judgment on the last day.

According to Jesus, He does not speak on His own authority but rather conveys the commandments and teachings given to Him by the Father, who sent Him. Jesus considers the Father's commandment to be eternal life, indicating that following His teachings leads to a life that transcends earthly existence.

The passage highlights the close relationship between Jesus and the Father, emphasizing that Jesus only speaks what the Father has told Him to say. It underscores Jesus' role as a messenger and representative of the Father, tasked with conveying divine truths to humanity.

Overall, these verses highlight the significance of accepting Jesus' teachings and understanding that they carry eternal importance. They also emphasize the unity and obedience between Jesus and the Father in their divine mission.

Chapter 13

Jesus' Love to the End

Now before the Feast of the Passover, Jesus knowing that His hour had come that He would depart out of this world to the Father, having loved His own who were in the world, He loved them to the end.

John 13:1 is a verse from the New Testament of the Bible, specifically from the Gospel of John. It describes the context leading up to the events of the Last Supper, which took place before the Feast of the Passover.

In this verse, it is mentioned that Jesus, having knowledge that His time had come to depart from this world and return to the Father (referring to His impending crucifixion and ascension), showed His love for His disciples who were in the world. It emphasizes that Jesus loved them until the very end.

This verse sets the stage for the subsequent events in the Gospel of John, where Jesus proceeds to wash His disciples' feet as an act of humility and teaches them important lessons about love and service. The events that follow in the Gospel include Jesus' betrayal, arrest, crucifixion, and resurrection.

Jesus' Humility at Last

During supper, the devil having already put into the heart of Judas Iscariot, the son of Simon, to betray Him, Jesus, knowing that the Father had given all things into His hands, and that He had come forth from God and was going back to God, got up from supper, and laid aside His garments; and taking a towel, He girded Himself.

John 13:2-4 describes an event during the Last Supper, where Jesus demonstrates an act of humility and service to His disciples. Let's break down the verses and understand their significance:

"During supper, the devil having already put into the heart of Judas Iscariot, the son of Simon, to betray Him..."

This verse highlights the presence of Judas Iscariot, one of Jesus' disciples, who had been influenced by Satan to betray Jesus. It signifies the fulfillment of Jesus' knowledge that one of His close followers would ultimately betray Him.

"Jesus, knowing that the Father had given all things into His hands, and that He had come forth from God and was going back to God..."

Here, Jesus is depicted as having complete awareness of His divine authority and His origin from God. He knows that His time on earth is coming to an end and that He will return to God the Father.

"Got up from supper, and laid aside His garments; and taking a towel, He girded Himself."

In an act of profound humility and servanthood, Jesus gets up from the table during the meal, removes His outer garments, and takes on the role of a servant by wrapping a towel around His waist. This act symbolizes His willingness to perform a task typically reserved for a lowly servant: washing the feet of His disciples.

The subsequent verses describe how Jesus proceeds to wash the feet of His disciples, including Judas, despite knowing that Judas would betray Him. This act serves as a powerful example of love, humility, and selflessness, encouraging His followers to serve one another and emphasizing the importance of humility in the Christian faith.

Jesus' Humble Foot-Washing

John 13:5-13, describes an incident where Jesus, during the Last Supper, humbly washes the feet of his disciples as an act of service and humility.

In this passage, Jesus takes on the role of a servant and performs the task of washing his disciples' feet. This act was typically done by a servant or a lower-ranking individual, so it was unexpected for Jesus, who was seen as their Teacher and Lord, to engage in such a humble act.

When Jesus approaches Simon Peter to wash his feet, Peter initially objects, not fully understanding the significance of Jesus' actions. However, Jesus tells Peter that if he does not allow Jesus to wash his feet, then Peter will have no part with him. Peter then asks Jesus to not only wash his feet but also his hands and head, indicating his desire to be completely cleansed by Jesus.

Jesus responds by explaining that those who have already bathed are clean but may still need to wash their feet. This can be understood both literally and symbolically. In a literal sense, Jesus is referring to the fact that after taking a bath, one's feet can become dirty while walking. Symbolically, Jesus is teaching that although the disciples have been cleansed spiritually, they still need to be humble and serve one another.

After washing their feet, Jesus explains to the disciples that by his actions, he has set an example for them to follow. He emphasizes that he is their Teacher and Lord, yet he performed the task of a servant. Therefore, they should also serve and humbly care for one another.

The act of foot-washing is often interpreted as a lesson in humility, love, and service. It teaches the importance of selflessness and putting others' needs above one's own. Jesus used this act to demonstrate the way his followers should treat one another, emphasizing the importance of serving others with love and humility.

This passage has had a significant impact on Christian traditions and is often practiced in some Christian communities as a symbolic act of humility and service, particularly during certain religious ceremonies, such as Maundy Thursday or Holy Thursday.

Teach & Model: Servant Leadership

For I gave you an example that you also should do as I did to you. Truly, truly, I say to you, a slave is not greater than his master, nor is one who is sent greater than the one who sent him. If you know these things, you are blessed if you do them. I do not speak of all of you. I know the ones I have chosen; but it is that the Scripture may be fulfilled, 'He who eats My bread has lifted up his heel against Me.' From now on I am telling you before it comes to pass, so that when it does occur, you may believe that I am He. Truly, truly, I say to you, he who receives whomever I send receives Me; and he who receives Me receives Him who sent Me."

In this passage from the Gospel of John (13:15-20), Jesus is speaking to his disciples during the Last Supper. He uses various statements to convey important teachings and reveal his identity and mission. Let's break down the key points:

"For I gave you an example that you also should do as I did to you."

Here, Jesus is emphasizing the importance of serving others. He had just washed the disciples' feet as an act of humility and service, setting an example for them to follow.

"Truly, truly, I say to you, a slave is not greater than his master, nor is one who is sent greater than the one who sent him."

Jesus is reminding the disciples that as his followers, they should not consider themselves above him or superior to him. He is their master and the one who sent them to carry out his mission.

"If you know these things, you are blessed if you do them."

Jesus emphasizes the importance of putting his teachings into action. He assures the disciples that they will be blessed if they not only understand his teachings but also live them out in their daily lives.

"I do not speak of all of you. I know the ones I have chosen; but it is that the Scripture may be fulfilled, 'He who eats My bread has lifted up his heel against Me.'"

Jesus acknowledges that not all of the disciples will follow his teachings faithfully. He refers to the prophecy in Scripture (Psalm

41:9) that predicts the betrayal of one who is close to him. This is a reference to Judas Iscariot, who later betrays Jesus.

"From now on, I am telling you before it comes to pass, so that when it does occur, you may believe that I am He."

Jesus is foretelling the betrayal by Judas before it happens. By predicting this event in advance, Jesus wants his disciples to understand that he has knowledge beyond human understanding, reinforcing his divine nature and the fulfillment of prophecy.

"Truly, truly, I say to you, he who receives whomever I send receives Me; and he who receives Me receives Him who sent Me."

Jesus establishes a principle of authority and representation. Those who accept and receive the messengers that Jesus sends are essentially accepting and receiving Jesus himself. Furthermore, by receiving Jesus, they are receiving God the Father who sent him.

Overall, this passage teaches the disciples about the importance of humility, service, and obedience to Jesus' teachings. It also emphasizes Jesus' divine authority and his role as the one sent by God.

Betrayal at Last Supper

When Jesus had said this, He became troubled in spirit, and testified and said, "Truly, truly, I say to you, that one of you will betray Me." The disciples began looking at one another, at a loss to know of which one He was speaking. There was reclining on Jesus' bosom one of His disciples, whom Jesus loved. So Simon Peter gestured to him, and said to him, "Tell us who it is of whom He is speaking." He, leaning back thus on Jesus' bosom, said to Him, "Lord, who is it?" Jesus then answered, "That is the one for whom I shall dip the morsel and give it to him." So when He had dipped the morsel, He took and gave it to Judas, the son of Simon Iscariot.

John 13:21-26. In this scene, Jesus is gathered with His disciples during the Last Supper. Jesus announces that one of them will betray

Him, causing the disciples to become troubled and confused, not knowing who among them Jesus is referring to.

During the meal, there is a disciple who is described as reclining on Jesus' bosom, which is a position of closeness and intimacy. This disciple is often referred to as the "disciple whom Jesus loved," and is traditionally understood to be the Apostle John.

Simon Peter, another disciple, gestures to the disciple whom Jesus loved and asks him to inquire about the identity of the betrayer. The disciple leans back against Jesus' chest and asks Him directly, "Lord, who is it?" Jesus then responds that the one He will give the dipped morsel to will be the betrayer.

Jesus dips a piece of bread or a morsel into a dish, likely a gesture of honor or friendship, and gives it to Judas Iscariot, the son of Simon, thus revealing him as the one who will betray Jesus.

This passage is significant because it marks the moment when Jesus publicly identifies Judas as the betrayer within the intimate setting of the Last Supper. It foreshadows the events that will follow, leading to Jesus' arrest, trial, and crucifixion.

Judas' betrayal and Jesus' glorification

After the morsel, Satan then entered into him. Therefore Jesus said to him, "What you do, do quickly." Now no one of those reclining at the table knew for what purpose He had said this to him. For some were supposing, because Judas had the money box, that Jesus was saying to him, "Buy the things we have need of for the feast"; or else, that he should give something to the poor. So after receiving the morsel he went out immediately; and it was night. Therefore when he had gone out, Jesus said, "Now is the Son of Man glorified, and God is glorified in Him; if God is glorified in Him, God will also glorify Him in Himself, and will glorify Him immediately.

In the passage of John 13:27-32, the events surrounding Judas Iscariot's betrayal of Jesus are described. Here's a breakdown of the events and the meaning behind Jesus' words:

"After the morsel, Satan then entered into him. Therefore Jesus said to him, 'What you do, do quickly.'" (John 13:27)

Judas had just received a piece of bread (the morsel) from Jesus during the Last Supper. After this, Satan influenced Judas, leading him to carry out his plan to betray Jesus.

Jesus, aware of Judas' intentions, tells him to proceed quickly with his betrayal.

"Now no one of those reclining at the table knew for what purpose He had said this to him." (John 13:28)

The other disciples present at the table did not understand the full significance of Jesus' words to Judas. They were unaware of Judas' plan to betray Jesus.

"For some were supposing, because Judas had the money box, that Jesus was saying to him, 'Buy the things we have need of for the feast'; or else, that he should give something to the poor." (John 13:29)

The disciples, speculating on the meaning of Jesus' words, thought that perhaps He had instructed Judas to purchase something for the upcoming Passover feast or to give something to the poor.

This shows that the disciples were not aware of Judas' true intentions.

"So after receiving the morsel he went out immediately, and it was night." (John 13:30)

Judas immediately left the gathering after taking the morsel from Jesus.

The mention that it was night signifies the darkness and secrecy surrounding Judas' betrayal.

"Therefore when he had gone out, Jesus said, 'Now is the Son of Man glorified, and God is glorified in Him.'" (John 13:31)

With Judas' departure, Jesus acknowledges that the time of His crucifixion and subsequent glorification is at hand.

Jesus refers to Himself as the Son of Man, a title associated with the Messiah.

"If God is glorified in Him, God will also glorify Him in Himself, and will glorify Him immediately." (John 13:32)

Jesus expresses that through His forthcoming suffering, death, and resurrection, God will be glorified.

This statement signifies the divine purpose behind Jesus' sacrificial act and the ultimate victory over sin and death.

In this passage, Jesus is aware of Judas' impending betrayal and acknowledges that the time has come for Him to fulfill His mission on Earth. While the disciples are initially unaware of Judas' true intentions, Jesus speaks of His glorification and the fulfillment of God's plan through His sacrificial death and resurrection.

Love Commandment and Disciples

Little children, I am with you a little while longer. You will seek Me; and as I said to the Jews, now I also say to you, 'Where I am going, you cannot come.' A new commandment I give to you, that you love one another, even as I have loved you, that you also love one another. By this all men will know that you are My disciples, if you have love for one another."

John 13:33-35 is a passage from the New Testament of the Bible, specifically from the Gospel of John. In this passage, Jesus is speaking to his disciples shortly before his crucifixion. Let's break down the verses and explore their meaning:

"Little children, I am with you a little while longer. You will seek Me; and as I said to the Jews, now I also say to you, 'Where I am going, you cannot come.'"

In these words, Jesus acknowledges that his time with his disciples is limited and that he will soon depart from them. He tells them that they will seek him, implying that they will desire to be with him, but he also explains that they cannot follow him to the place he is going. Jesus is referring to his impending death, resurrection, and ascension to heaven, which his disciples will not experience at that moment.

"A new commandment I give to you, that you love one another, even as I have loved you, that you also love one another."

Here, Jesus presents his disciples with a new commandment. While the concept of loving one's neighbor existed in Jewish teachings, Jesus takes it further by emphasizing a radical kind of love. He instructs his disciples to love one another as he has loved them. This love is characterized by selflessness, sacrificial action, and unconditional care for others.

"By this all men will know that you are My disciples, if you have love for one another."

Jesus states that the way his disciples demonstrate their allegiance to him is through their love for one another. He highlights the importance of love as a distinguishing characteristic of his followers. The depth and quality of their love for each other will serve as a testimony to the world, revealing that they are truly disciples of Jesus.

In summary, these verses emphasize the imminent departure of Jesus from his disciples and the commandment he gives them to love one another in the same way he has loved them. This love serves as a defining characteristic of his followers, a witness to the world of their relationship with Jesus.

Peter's Denial Predicted

Simon Peter said to Him, "Lord, where are You going?" Jesus answered, "Where I go, you cannot follow Me now; but you will follow later." Peter said to Him, "Lord, why can I not follow You right now? I will lay down my life for You." Jesus answered, "Will you lay down your life for Me? Truly, truly, I say to you, a rooster will not crow until you deny Me three times.

In this passage from the Gospel of John (John 13:36-38), Simon Peter asks Jesus where He is going. Jesus responds by saying that Peter cannot follow Him at that moment, but he will be able to follow Him later. Peter insists that he is willing to lay down his life for Jesus, but Jesus predicts that Peter will deny Him three times before the rooster crows.

This exchange between Peter and Jesus takes place during the Last Supper, shortly before Jesus' arrest and crucifixion. Jesus is preparing His disciples for His impending departure and trying to convey important teachings to them. Peter, known for his impulsive nature and deep devotion to Jesus, expresses his desire to follow Him wherever He goes, even to the point of sacrificing his own life.

However, Jesus responds by indicating that Peter is not yet ready to follow Him in the way he intends. Jesus knows that Peter will face a test of his faith and loyalty, and he foretells Peter's denial. Despite Peter's sincere intentions, he will falter and deny Jesus three times before the rooster crows in the morning.

This conversation serves as a foreshadowing of the events that will unfold. Later in the Gospel of John, Peter does indeed deny Jesus three times, as Jesus predicted. These denials occur when Peter is questioned about his association with Jesus during the time of Jesus' trial and crucifixion.

Ultimately, Peter's denial is a moment of weakness and fear, but it also sets the stage for his eventual repentance and restoration. After Jesus' resurrection, He appears to Peter and restores their relationship, emphasizing the importance of love and loyalty. Peter goes on to become a key figure in the early Christian movement, displaying great courage and leadership.

Chapter 14

Comfort and guidance

"Do not let your heart be troubled; believe in God, believe also in Me. In My Father's house are many dwelling places; if it were not so, I would have told you; for I go to prepare a place for you. If I go and prepare a place for you, I will come again and receive you to Myself, that where I am, there you may be also. And you know the way where I am going." Thomas said to Him, "Lord, we do not know where You are going, how do we know the way?" Jesus said to him, "I am the way, and the truth, and the life; no one comes to the Father but through Me.

John 14:1-6 is a passage from the Bible where Jesus is speaking to His disciples, providing them with comfort and guidance. Let's break down the key points of this passage:

"Do not let your heart be troubled; believe in God, believe also in Me." Here, Jesus encourages His disciples not to be troubled or anxious but to place their trust in both God and Himself. He is reassuring them that they can find peace and solace in their faith.

"In My Father's house are many dwelling places; if it were not so, I would have told you; for I go to prepare a place for you." Jesus is telling His disciples that there are many rooms or dwelling places in His Father's house (Heaven). He is assuring them that He is going ahead to prepare a place for them, indicating that there is a future hope and eternal life with God.

"If I go and prepare a place for you, I will come again and receive you to Myself, that where I am, there you may be also." Jesus promises that He will return to gather His followers to Himself so that they can be with Him where He is. This statement speaks of Jesus' second coming and the hope of being united with Him in the future.

Thomas expresses his confusion, saying, "Lord, we do not know where You are going, how do we know the way?" Thomas doesn't understand the destination Jesus is referring to or how to reach it.

Jesus responds to Thomas, saying, "I am the way, and the truth, and the life; no one comes to the Father but through Me." Here, Jesus reveals that He Himself is the way to the Father, the source of truth, and the giver of eternal life. He emphasizes that no one can come to God the Father except through Him, suggesting that a personal relationship with Jesus is essential for salvation.

In summary, this passage conveys Jesus' comforting words to His disciples, assuring them of His role in preparing a place for them in Heaven, promising His return, and declaring Himself as the way to the Father. It emphasizes the importance of trust in God and Jesus and the belief in Jesus as the path to eternal life.

Knowing Jesus, Knowing Father.

If you had known Me, you would have known My Father also; from now on you know Him, and have seen Him." Philip said to Him, "Lord, show us the Father, and it is enough for us." Jesus said to him, "Have I been so long with you, and yet you have not come to know Me, Philip? He who has seen Me has seen the Father; how can you say, 'Show us the Father'? Do you not believe that I am in the Father, and the Father is in Me? The words that I say to you I do not speak on My own initiative, but the Father abiding in Me does His works. Believe Me that I am in the Father and the Father is in Me; otherwise believe because of the works themselves. Truly, truly, I say to you, he who believes in Me, the works that I do, he will do also; and greater works than these he will do; because I go to the Father. Whatever you ask in My name, that will I do, so that the Father may be glorified in the Son. If you ask Me anything in My name, I will do it. "If you love Me, you will keep My commandments.

In this passage from John 14:7-15, Jesus is addressing His disciples, particularly Philip, who has asked Him to show them the

Father. Jesus responds by explaining the close relationship between Himself and the Father.

Jesus begins by expressing that if His disciples had known Him, they would have known the Father as well. He emphasizes that from that point onward, they have come to know the Father and have seen Him through knowing Jesus Himself.

Philip then requests Jesus to show them the Father, to which Jesus responds with a gentle rebuke. Jesus wonders why, after spending so much time with Him, Philip still doesn't understand that seeing Jesus is equivalent to seeing the Father. Jesus further explains that He and the Father are inseparable, with the Father dwelling in Him and doing His works through Him. Jesus encourages Philip and the other disciples to believe in Him based on His words and works.

Moreover, Jesus assures His disciples that those who believe in Him will also do the works that He has done, and even greater works, because He is going to the Father. He promises that whatever they ask in His name, He will do, so that the Father may be glorified through Him. Jesus reiterates that if they love Him, they will keep His commandments.

In summary, Jesus uses this passage to emphasize His unity with the Father and the importance of knowing Him to truly know the Father. He encourages His disciples to believe in Him based on His words and works, and He promises that those who believe in Him will do great works as well. Additionally, Jesus reminds them that keeping His commandments is a demonstration of their love for Him.

Holy Spirit Promised Helper

I will ask the Father, and He will give you another Helper, that He may be with you forever; that is the Spirit of truth, whom the world cannot receive, because it does not see Him or know Him, but you know Him because He abides with you and will be in you. "I will not leave you as orphans; I will come to you. After a little while the world will no longer see Me, but you will see Me; because I live, you will live also. In that day you will know that I am in My Father, and you in Me, and I in you. He who has My commandments and keeps them is the one who loves Me; and he who loves Me will be loved by My Father, and I will love him and will disclose Myself to him."

The passage you mentioned, John 16:16-22, is part of a larger discourse where Jesus is preparing his disciples for his impending departure. In these verses, Jesus promises to send the Holy Spirit as another Helper or Advocate who will be with his disciples forever. This Helper is referred to as the Spirit of truth, and the world cannot receive Him because it neither sees Him nor knows Him.

Jesus assures his disciples that he will not leave them as orphans but will come to them. He acknowledges that for a little while, the world will no longer see him, but his disciples will see him because he lives and they will also live. This can be understood as a reference to his resurrection and the spiritual presence he will have with his followers.

On that day, the disciples will know that Jesus is in the Father, and they are in him, and he is in them. This speaks to the intimate relationship between Jesus, the Father, and his disciples. Jesus emphasizes the importance of keeping his commandments as an expression of love for him. Those who love him and keep his commandments will be loved by the Father, and Jesus promises to love them and reveal himself to them.

Overall, this passage speaks of Jesus' departure, the coming of the Holy Spirit as a permanent Helper, and the deep connection and love shared between Jesus, the Father, and his disciples. It also highlights the importance of obedience to Jesus' commandments as an expression of love for him.

John m14:22-31 Love, Obedience, Holy Spirit

Judas (not Iscariot) said to Him, "Lord, what then has happened that You are going to disclose Yourself to us and not to the world?" Jesus answered and said to him, "If anyone loves Me, he will keep My word; and My Father will love him, and We will come to him and make Our abode with him. He who does not love Me does not keep My words; and the word which you hear is not Mine, but the Father's who sent Me. "These things I have spoken to you while abiding with you. But the Helper, the Holy Spirit, whom the Father will send in My name, He will teach you all things, and bring to your remembrance all that I said to you. Peace I leave with you; My peace I give to you; not as the world gives do I give to you. Do not let your heart be troubled, nor let it be fearful. You heard that I said to you, 'I go away, and I will come to you.' If you loved Me, you would have rejoiced because I go to the Father, for the Father is greater than I. Now I have told you before it happens, so that when it happens, you may believe. I will not speak much more with you, for the ruler of the world is coming, and he has nothing in Me; but so that the world may know that I love the Father, I do exactly as the Father commanded Me. Get up, let us go from here.

In this passage from John 14:22-31, Judas (not Iscariot) asks Jesus why He is going to disclose Himself to His disciples but not to the world. Jesus responds by explaining that those who love Him and keep His word will receive the love of the Father, and both Jesus and the Father will come and make their abode with them. On the other hand, those who do not love Jesus do not keep His words. Jesus emphasizes that His teachings are not His own but come from the Father who sent Him.

Jesus reassures His disciples that He has spoken these things while being with them. He promises them the Holy Spirit, the Helper, who will be sent by the Father in His name. The Holy Spirit will teach them all things and bring to their remembrance everything Jesus said to them.

Jesus then speaks about leaving His peace with His disciples and giving it to them, but not in the way that the world gives. He encourages them not to let their hearts be troubled or fearful. He reminds them of His earlier statement about going away and coming back to them, explaining that if they truly loved Him, they would have rejoiced because He is going to the Father, who is greater than Him. Jesus reveals that He has foretold these events so that when they happen, His disciples may believe.

Jesus tells His disciples that He will not speak much more with them because the ruler of the world is coming, but reassures them that this ruler has no power over Him. He explains that He does the Father's commandments to demonstrate His love for the Father. Finally, Jesus concludes by urging His disciples to get up and go from there.

This passage emphasizes the importance of love for Jesus and obedience to His words, as well as the promise of the Holy Spirit as a guide and teacher. It also highlights Jesus' imminent departure, the coming of the Holy Spirit, and the assurance of peace in the midst of trouble.

Chapter 15

Vine and Branches

"I am the true vine, and My Father is the vinedresser. Every branch in Me that does not bear fruit, He takes away; and every branch that bears fruit, He prunes it so that it may bear more fruit.

John 15:1-2 is a passage from the Bible in which Jesus uses the metaphor of a vine and branches to teach about the relationship between himself, his followers, and God the Father. Let's break down the meaning of these verses:

"I am the true vine, and My Father is the vinedresser."

In this statement, Jesus refers to himself as the true vine. The vine is a metaphor for the source of life and nourishment for the branches, which represent his followers. By calling himself the true vine, Jesus emphasizes that he is the authentic and genuine source of spiritual life. He also acknowledges the role of God the Father as the vinedresser, who tends to the vineyard and cares for the branches.

"Every branch in Me that does not bear fruit, He takes away; and every branch that bears fruit, He prunes it so that it may bear more fruit."

In this part of the passage, Jesus describes the two possible conditions of the branches: those that bear fruit and those that do not. The branches that do not bear fruit are taken away by the Father. This can be understood as a reference to individuals who may profess faith or claim to be followers of Jesus but do not produce the evidence of a transformed life or spiritual fruit.

On the other hand, the branches that do bear fruit are pruned by the vinedresser. Pruning involves cutting off unnecessary or unproductive parts of the branch to promote growth and increase fruitfulness. This can be seen as a metaphor for the Father's discipline and purification of believers through various means, such as trials, challenges, and correction. The purpose of this pruning is to enhance the spiritual growth and fruit-bearing capacity of the branch.

Overall, this passage teaches that Jesus is the true source of spiritual life, and God the Father tends to his followers as a vinedresser tends to a vineyard. The Father removes branches that do not bear fruit and prunes those that do, aiming to cultivate greater fruitfulness and spiritual growth among believers.

Cleaned by Jesus's Word

You are already clean because of the word which I have spoken to you.

John 15:3 is a verse from the New Testament of the Bible, specifically from the book of John. In this verse, Jesus is speaking to his disciples and says, "You are already clean because of the word which I have spoken to you." Let's explore the meaning of this verse.

In the context of John 15, Jesus is using the analogy of a vine and its branches to illustrate the relationship between himself (the vine) and his disciples (the branches). He emphasizes the importance of remaining connected to him to bear fruit and live a fruitful life.

When Jesus says, "You are already clean because of the word which I have spoken to you," he is referring to the spiritual cleansing and purification that has taken place in the lives of his disciples through his teachings and message. The "word" here represents the teachings of Jesus, his commandments, and the truth he has shared with his followers.

Jesus is implying that through their acceptance of his teachings and their faith in him, his disciples have experienced a cleansing of their hearts and souls. It means that they have been forgiven of their sins and have been made spiritually clean or pure. This cleansing comes from the transformative power of Jesus' words and his role as the Savior.

By stating that they are "already clean," Jesus affirms that his disciples have undergone this purification process. It suggests that they have received forgiveness, redemption, and a new spiritual standing through their relationship with him.

Furthermore, this verse also highlights the ongoing importance of Jesus' teachings in the lives of his followers. It reminds them that they should continue to abide in his word, remain connected to him, and allow his teachings to shape their thoughts, actions, and character.

Overall, John 15:3 conveys the message that through faith in Jesus and acceptance of his teachings, his disciples have experienced spiritual cleansing and purification. It emphasizes the significance of abiding in his word and allowing his teachings to continue to guide and transform their lives.

Abiding in Jesus' Fruitfulness.

Abide in Me, and I in you. As the branch cannot bear fruit of itself unless it abides in the vine, so neither can you unless you abide in Me. I am the vine, you are the branches; he who abides in Me and I in him, he bears much fruit, for apart from Me you can do nothing. If anyone does not abide in Me, he is thrown away as a branch and dries up; and they gather them, and cast them into the fire and they are burned. If you abide in Me, and My words abide in you, ask whatever you wish, and it will be done for you. My Father is glorified by this, that you bear much fruit, and so prove to be My disciples.

John 15:4-8 is a passage from the Bible in which Jesus uses the metaphor of a vine and its branches to illustrate the relationship between believers and himself. Let's break down the meaning of these verses:

"Abide in Me, and I in you. As the branch cannot bear fruit of itself unless it abides in the vine, so neither can you unless you abide in Me."

Here, Jesus emphasizes the importance of remaining connected to him. Just as a branch cannot bear fruit unless it remains attached to the vine, believers cannot bear spiritual fruit unless they remain connected to Jesus. This connection is a two-way relationship, as Jesus also says, "and I in you," highlighting the intimate nature of this connection.

"I am the vine, you are the branches; he who abides in Me and I in him, he bears much fruit, for apart from Me you can do nothing."

Jesus identifies himself as the vine, and believers as the branches. The branches derive their life, nourishment, and ability to bear fruit from the vine. Jesus emphasizes that apart from him, believers can do nothing of spiritual significance. True fruitfulness and productivity in the Christian life come from staying closely connected to Jesus and relying on him.

"If anyone does not abide in Me, he is thrown away as a branch and dries up; and they gather them, and cast them into the fire and they are burned."

This verse warns of the consequences of not abiding in Jesus. Those who do not remain connected to him spiritually are like withered branches that are gathered and thrown into the fire. It signifies the spiritual death and judgment that come from separation from Christ.

"If you abide in Me, and My words abide in you, ask whatever you wish, and it will be done for you."

Jesus promises that if believers abide in him and his words remain in them, they will have their prayers answered. This is not a carte blanche to ask for anything without regard to God's will, but rather an assurance that prayers aligned with God's purposes and will, arising from an intimate relationship with Jesus, will be granted.

"My Father is glorified by this, that you bear much fruit, and so prove to be My disciples."

Jesus reveals that by bearing much fruit, believers bring glory to God the Father. Fruitfulness in the Christian life, which includes traits like love, joy, peace, patience, kindness, goodness, faithfulness, gentleness, and self-control, serves as evidence of being Jesus' disciples.

Overall, these verses emphasize the importance of remaining connected to Jesus, relying on him for spiritual nourishment, and bearing fruit that brings glory to God. It highlights the transformative power of abiding in Christ and the significance of a vibrant relationship with him for a fruitful Christian life.

Love, Obedience, Joy

Just as the Father has loved Me, I have also loved you; abide in My love. If you keep My commandments, you will abide in My love; just as I have kept My Father's commandments and abide in His love. These things I have spoken to you so that My joy may be in you, and that your joy may be made full.

In John 15:9-11, Jesus is speaking to His disciples and conveying important teachings about love, obedience, and joy. Let's break down the verses and explore their meaning:

Verse 9: "Just as the Father has loved Me, I have also loved you; abide in My love."

Here, Jesus emphasizes the love that exists between Him and His disciples. He draws a parallel between the love He receives from the Father and the love He extends to His followers. He urges them to remain, or abide, in His love. This implies that they should dwell in His love, seeking a close and enduring relationship with Him.

Verse 10: "If you keep My commandments, you will abide in My love; just as I have kept My Father's commandments and abide in His love."

Jesus emphasizes the importance of obedience as a way to abide in His love. He states that by keeping His commandments, His disciples will continue to experience and remain in His love. Jesus sets an example by highlighting His own obedience to the Father's commandments and how it enables Him to abide in the Father's love.

Verse 11: "These things I have spoken to you so that My joy may be in you, and that your joy may be made full."

Jesus explains that He has shared these teachings so that His joy may be present within His disciples. By following His words, they can experience a fullness of joy. Jesus wants His followers to embrace His teachings, find joy in their relationship with Him, and live according to His commandments.

Overall, this passage conveys the interconnectedness of love, obedience, and joy. Jesus emphasizes the love He has for His disciples, encourages them to abide in His love through obedience, and promises that by doing so, they will experience a profound joy.

Love, Friendship, and Obedience

This is My commandment, that you love one another, just as I have loved you. Greater love has no one than this, that one lay down his life for his friends. You are My friends if you do what I command you. No longer do I call you slaves, for the slave does not know what his master is doing; but I have called you friends, for all things that I have heard from My Father I have made known to you.

John 15:12-15 is a passage from the New Testament of the Bible, specifically from the Gospel of John. In these verses, Jesus is speaking to his disciples, conveying important teachings about love and friendship.

Let's break down the passage:

"This is My commandment, that you love one another, just as I have loved you." Here, Jesus is giving his disciples a new commandment, emphasizing the importance of love. He instructs them to love one another, not just in a general sense but as Jesus himself has loved them. Jesus's love is selfless, sacrificial, and unconditional, and he expects his disciples to demonstrate the same kind of love towards one another.

"Greater love has no one than this, that one lay down his life for his friends." In this statement, Jesus emphasizes the highest expression of love, which is to lay down one's life for one's friends. Jesus himself would later demonstrate this ultimate act of love by willingly giving up his life on the cross for the salvation of humanity. This verse highlights the depth and magnitude of Jesus's love for his disciples and all humanity.

"You are My friends if you do what I command you." Jesus distinguishes his disciples from slaves, referring to them as his friends. He states that they become his friends if they follow his commandments. Jesus invites his disciples into a deep, personal relationship with him, where they are not merely servants but trusted friends. Friendship with Jesus involves obedience to his teachings and a willingness to follow his example.

"No longer do I call you slaves, for the slave does not know what his master is doing; but I have called you friends, for all things that I have heard from My Father I have made known to you." Jesus contrasts the relationship between a master and a slave with the relationship he has with his disciples. Slaves are kept in the dark about their master's plans, but Jesus has shared everything he has heard from the Father with his disciples. He has revealed to them the truths of God's kingdom, his purpose, and his teachings, treating them as trusted confidants.

In summary, John 15:12-15 teaches that love is a central commandment for Jesus's disciples. He calls them to love one another with the same selfless love he has shown them. By following his commandments and being obedient, the disciples enter into a deep friendship with Jesus. This friendship is characterized by a mutual exchange of knowledge and intimacy, where Jesus reveals the truths he has received from the Father to his disciples.

Chosen to Bear Fruit

You did not choose Me but I chose you, and appointed you that you would go and bear fruit, and that your fruit would remain, so that whatever you ask of the Father in My name He may give to you. This I command you, that you love one another.

John 15:16-17 is a passage from the Bible where Jesus is speaking to his disciples. Let's break down the verses:

"You did not choose Me, but I chose you, and appointed you that you would go and bear fruit, and that your fruit would remain."

In this verse, Jesus is emphasizing that it was He who chose his disciples, rather than the other way around. He appointed them with a specific purpose, which was to go and bear fruit. The fruit refers to the results of their ministry, such as spreading the message of the Gospel and making disciples. Jesus also emphasizes that the fruit should remain, indicating the lasting impact and influence of their work.

"So that whatever you ask of the Father in My name He may give to you."

Jesus promises that if his disciples ask anything of the Father in his name, it will be given to them. This highlights the special relationship between the disciples and God the Father through Jesus. By praying in Jesus' name, they have the assurance that their requests will be granted according to God's will.

"This I command you, that you love one another."

In this final statement, Jesus commands his disciples to love one another. Love is a central theme in Jesus' teachings, and he emphasizes the importance of loving others as a fundamental aspect of following him. By loving one another, the disciples would demonstrate their commitment to Jesus and reflect the love that he has shown them.

Overall, these verses convey the message that Jesus has chosen and appointed his disciples for a specific purpose. They are called to bear fruit, to have a lasting impact in their ministry. They can approach God with confidence in prayer, knowing that their requests will be heard and answered. Lastly, Jesus commands them to love one another, which is an essential aspect of their discipleship and a reflection of their relationship with him.

Hated for Following Jesus

John 15:18-27, is part of Jesus' farewell discourse to his disciples. In this passage, Jesus prepares his disciples for the opposition and persecution they will face as his followers. He tells them that if the world hates them, it is because the world hated him first. Jesus explains that because his disciples are not of the world but have been chosen by him, the world will hate them.

Jesus reminds his disciples that he is their master and that if he faced persecution, they should expect the same treatment. He emphasizes that those who persecute them do not know the One who sent Jesus, which is God the Father. Jesus states that his coming and his teachings have made people accountable for their sins because they have rejected him and his Father.

Furthermore, Jesus mentions that the world's hatred toward him and his Father is in fulfillment of what was written in the Law, specifically referring to Psalm 69:4, which states, "Those who hate me without a cause are more than the hairs of my head."

However, Jesus assures his disciples that they will not be left alone. He promises to send them the Helper, the Spirit of truth, who will testify about him and empower them to testify as well. The disciples have been with Jesus from the beginning of his ministry and will bear witness to his life, teachings, and resurrection.

In summary, this passage highlights the reality of opposition and persecution that Jesus' followers may face in the world. It also emphasizes the role of the Holy Spirit in supporting and enabling them to testify about Jesus and his message.

Chapter 16

Warned of Persecution.

"These things I have spoken to you so that you may be kept from stumbling. They will make you outcasts from the synagogue, but an hour is coming for everyone who kills you to think that he is offering service to God. These things they will do because they have not known the Father or Me. But these things I have spoken to you, so that when their hour comes, you may remember that I told you of them. These things I did not say to you at the beginning, because I was with you".

In John 16:1-4, Jesus is speaking to his disciples and warning them about the challenges they will face as his followers. He tells them that he is sharing these things with them so that they may be kept from stumbling or falling away from their faith.

Jesus foretells that his disciples will face persecution and rejection from the religious establishment of the time, symbolized by being outcasts from the synagogue. He warns that a time will come when those who oppose the disciples may even resort to violence and killing, believing that they are serving God by doing so.

However, Jesus explains that the reason for this opposition is a lack of knowledge and understanding. Those who persecute the disciples do not truly know God the Father or Jesus Himself. Jesus emphasizes that he is sharing these things with his disciples in advance so that when the time comes, they will remember that he had warned them.

Jesus states that he had not revealed these things earlier because he was physically present with his disciples, providing them with guidance and protection. But now that his departure is imminent, he wants to prepare them for the challenges they will face in his absence.

Overall, this passage highlights the reality of persecution and rejection that Jesus' followers may encounter, but also assures them that Jesus has forewarned them and that they can find strength and resilience in remembering his words.

Understanding John 16:5-11

But now I am going to Him who sent Me; and none of you asks Me, 'Where are You going?' But because I have said these things to you, sorrow has filled your heart. But I tell you the truth, it is to your advantage that I go away; for if I do not go away, the Helper will not come to you; but if I go, I will send Him to you. And He, when He comes, will convict the world concerning sin and righteousness and judgment; concerning sin, because they do not believe in Me; and concerning righteousness, because I go to the Father and you no longer see Me; and concerning judgment, because the ruler of this world has been judged.

In John 16:5-11, Jesus is speaking to His disciples before His crucifixion and resurrection. He addresses their sorrow and explains the purpose and advantage of His departure. Let's break down the passage and discuss its key points:

"But now I am going to Him who sent Me; and none of you asks Me, 'Where are You going?' But because I have said these things to you, sorrow has filled your heart."

Here, Jesus acknowledges that His disciples have not asked Him where He is going, but they are saddened by His words. They are concerned and troubled by the idea of Him leaving them.

"But I tell you the truth, it is to your advantage that I go away; for if I do not go away, the Helper will not come to you; but if I go, I will send Him to you."

Jesus assures His disciples that His departure is actually advantageous for them. He explains that if He does not go away, the Helper (referring to the Holy Spirit) will not come to them. However, if He goes, He will send the Helper to them. The coming of the Holy Spirit would bring significant benefits and empower them.

"And He, when He comes, will convict the world concerning sin and righteousness and judgment."

Jesus explains that the Helper, the Holy Spirit, will fulfill a specific role. When He comes, He will convict the world in three areas: sin, righteousness, and judgment.

"Concerning sin, because they do not believe in Me."

The Holy Spirit will convict the world of sin, primarily the sin of not believing in Jesus. The Holy Spirit works in people's hearts to bring conviction and awareness of their need for salvation through faith in Christ.

"And concerning righteousness, because I go to the Father and you no longer see Me."

The Holy Spirit will also convict the world concerning righteousness. Jesus' departure to the Father signifies His victory over sin and death, and the Holy Spirit's presence will testify to this righteousness.

"And concerning judgment, because the ruler of this world has been judged."

The Holy Spirit will convict the world concerning judgment, as the ruler of this world (referring to Satan) has already been judged through Jesus' sacrificial death and resurrection. The Holy Spirit will reveal this truth and demonstrate the ultimate victory of Christ over the powers of darkness.

In summary, Jesus explains to His disciples that His departure is necessary for the coming of the Holy Spirit. The Holy Spirit will fulfill a crucial role in convicting the world of sin, righteousness, and judgment. The Holy Spirit's work would bring about a deeper understanding of faith, righteousness, and the victory accomplished through Jesus' sacrifice.

Spirit Guides into Truth

"I have many more things to say to you, but you cannot bear them now. But when He, the Spirit of truth, comes, He will guide you into all the truth; for He will not speak on His own initiative, but whatever He hears, He will speak; and He will disclose to you what is to come. He will glorify Me, for He will take of Mine and will disclose it to you. All things that the Father has are Mine; therefore I said that He takes of Mine and will disclose it to you".

The passage of John 16:12-15, is part of Jesus' farewell discourse to his disciples before his crucifixion. In these verses, Jesus speaks about the coming of the "Spirit of truth," referring to the Holy Spirit, who would guide the disciples and reveal further truths to them.

According to the passage, Jesus tells his disciples that there are still many things he wants to teach them, but they are not ready to bear those teachings at that moment. However, when the Spirit of truth comes, he will guide them into all truth. This means that the Holy Spirit will provide the disciples with the understanding and insight they need to comprehend deeper spiritual truths and revelations.

Furthermore, Jesus emphasizes that the Holy Spirit will not speak on his own initiative but will convey what he hears. This indicates that the Holy Spirit will communicate the messages and teachings that originate from God the Father.

The passage also states that the Spirit of truth will disclose what is to come. This suggests that the Holy Spirit will reveal future events and give the disciples knowledge and understanding about the unfolding of God's plan.

Moreover, the Holy Spirit will glorify Jesus. He will take what belongs to Jesus and disclose it to the disciples. This highlights the role of the Holy Spirit in illuminating the truth about Jesus and pointing people towards him.

In summary, John 16:12-15 conveys Jesus' assurance to his disciples that the Holy Spirit will continue to guide and teach them after his departure. The Holy Spirit will reveal deeper truths, disclose future events, glorify Jesus, and transmit the teachings that originate from God the Father.

Confusion about Jesus' departure

In the passage from John 16:16-22, Jesus is speaking to his disciples and preparing them for his impending departure. He uses the phrase, "A little while, and you will no longer see Me; and again a little while, and you will see Me," which confuses the disciples. They are unsure about what Jesus means by this statement and why he is talking about going to the Father.

Jesus, being aware of their confusion, addresses their concerns. He acknowledges their desire to question him and clarifies the meaning behind his words. He explains that they will experience a time of sorrow and mourning when he is no longer physically present with them, but their grief will be turned into joy. Jesus uses the analogy of a woman in labor to illustrate this idea. A woman experiences pain and anguish during childbirth, but once the child is born, her pain is replaced by the joy of new life.

Similarly, Jesus tells his disciples that they will experience sorrow when he is crucified and taken from them. However, their sorrow will be transformed into joy when they see him again after his resurrection. He assures them that their joy will be permanent and cannot be taken away by anyone.

This passage foreshadows Jesus' death, resurrection, and the subsequent joy that his disciples will experience when they witness his resurrection and the establishment of the Kingdom of God. It serves to prepare the disciples for the challenges they will face, reminding them that their temporary sorrow will be followed by everlasting joy in the presence of the resurrected Jesus.

Praying in Jesus' Name

In John 16:23-33, Jesus is speaking to His disciples, preparing them for His departure and the challenges they will face. He begins by saying that in a future time, they will not need to question Him about anything because they will have a direct connection with the Father through prayer in Jesus' name. He assures them that if they ask the Father for anything in His name, the Father will grant their requests. This is a significant shift because up until that point, the disciples had not asked the Father directly in Jesus' name.

Jesus then explains that He has been speaking to them in figurative language, but a time is coming when He will speak plainly about the Father. He tells them that when that time comes, they will be able to ask in His name directly to the Father, and Jesus Himself will not need to make requests on their behalf. Jesus emphasizes that the Father loves them because they have loved Him and believed in His divine origin. He came from the Father into the world and is now returning to the Father.

The disciples acknowledge that Jesus is speaking plainly and recognize His divine knowledge. They express their belief that Jesus came from God. Jesus responds by questioning their current level of belief and warns them that they will soon be scattered, leaving Him alone. Despite their abandonment, Jesus assures them that He is not truly alone because the Father is with Him.

Jesus concludes by telling His disciples that He has spoken these things to them so that they may have peace in Him. He acknowledges that they will face tribulations in the world but encourages them to take courage because He has overcome the world.

This passage highlights the disciples' transition from relying on Jesus' physical presence to having a direct relationship with the Father through prayer in Jesus' name. It also foreshadows the challenges they will face and the assurance that Jesus will be with them even in His physical absence. Additionally, Jesus emphasizes the importance of believing in Him and the peace that can be found in Him despite the difficulties of the world.

Chapter 17

Jesus Prays for Glory

Jesus spoke these things; and lifting up His eyes to heaven, He said, "Father, the hour has come; glorify Your Son, that the Son may glorify You, even as You gave Him authority over all flesh, that to all whom You have given Him, He may give eternal life. This is eternal life, that they may know You, the only true God, and Jesus Christ whom You have sent. I glorified You on the earth, having accomplished the work which You have given Me to do. Now, Father, glorify Me together with Yourself, with the glory which I had with You before the world was.

John 17:1-5 is a passage from the Bible, specifically from the Gospel of John in the New Testament. In these verses, Jesus is praying to God the Father shortly before his crucifixion. He begins by acknowledging that the time has come for him to be glorified so that he may, in turn, glorify the Father. Jesus speaks about the authority given to him over all flesh, indicating his divine role as the Son of God.

Jesus then expresses his desire to give eternal life to those whom God has given him. He defines eternal life as knowing the Father, who is the only true God, and Jesus Christ, whom the Father has sent. Here, Jesus emphasizes the importance of knowing God personally as the path to eternal life.

Continuing his prayer, Jesus affirms that he has glorified God on earth by accomplishing the work that God gave him to do. He speaks of the completion of his mission on earth, likely referring to his teaching, miracles, and ultimately his impending sacrifice on the cross.

Finally, Jesus requests that the Father glorify him with the same glory they shared before the world existed. This statement alludes to the preexistence of Jesus with the Father and highlights the unity and divine nature of their relationship.

Overall, this passage portrays Jesus' intimate conversation with God the Father, expressing his desire for mutual glorification, his role as the giver of eternal life, his completion of the work assigned to him, and his longing to return to the glory he shared with the Father before his earthly ministry.

Praying for Disciples' Unit

John 17:6-12 is a passage from the New Testament in which Jesus is praying to God the Father on behalf of his disciples. Let's break down the key points in this passage:

Jesus acknowledges that he has revealed and made known God's name to the disciples who were given to him by God: "I have manifested Your name to the men whom You gave Me out of the world; they were Yours and You gave them to Me, and they have kept Your word."

The disciples have come to understand that everything Jesus has received is from God, and they have received and understood the words given to them by Jesus: "Now they have come to know that everything You have given Me is from You; for the words which You gave Me I have given to them; and they received them and truly understood that I came forth from You, and they believed that You sent Me."

Jesus asks God to protect and keep the disciples in His name, so that they may be united as one, just as Jesus and God the Father are one: "Holy Father, keep them in Your name, the name which You have given Me, that they may be one even as We are."

Jesus acknowledges that he has glorified God through his disciples: "And I have been glorified in them."

Jesus mentions that he is no longer in the world, but his disciples are still in the world, and he prays for their protection and unity: "I am no longer in the world; and yet they themselves are in the world, and I come to You."

Jesus recalls that during his time with the disciples, he kept them in God's name and guarded them, and only one of them, the son of perdition (referring to Judas Iscariot), perished in order to fulfill the Scriptures: "While I was with them, I was keeping them in Your name which You have given Me; and I guarded them and not one of them perished but the son of perdition, so that the Scripture would be fulfilled."

In this passage, Jesus expresses his deep concern for the well-being, unity, and protection of his disciples and prays to God the Father on their behalf. He acknowledges their faithfulness, asks for their continued safety, and recognizes that they are to carry on in the world while he returns to the Father.

Jesus' Prayer for Unity

John 17:13-20 is part of Jesus' prayer to God the Father, often referred to as the "High Priestly Prayer." In this passage, Jesus prays for His disciples and all future believers, emphasizing their separation from the world and their unity in faith.

In verse 13, Jesus expresses His desire for His disciples to experience complete joy, a joy that comes from their relationship with Him. He wants them to have His joy made full in themselves.

Jesus acknowledges that His disciples are not of the world, just as He Himself is not of the world (verse 14). The world, representing the fallen and sinful state of humanity, is hostile towards Jesus and His followers. The disciples' commitment to Christ and His teachings sets them apart from the values and behaviors of the world, resulting in the world's hatred towards them.

However, Jesus does not pray for His disciples to be taken out of the world (verse 15). Instead, He asks God to protect them from the evil one, referring to Satan. Jesus recognizes that His followers have a mission to fulfill in the world, and their presence is necessary to spread the message of salvation.

In verse 17, Jesus prays for the sanctification of His disciples. To sanctify means to set apart or make holy. Jesus asks God to set His disciples apart through the truth, which is the Word of God. The Word of God, revealed through Jesus, is truth itself.

Jesus draws a parallel between His own mission and that of His disciples in verse 18. Just as the Father sent Jesus into the world, Jesus now sends His disciples into the world to continue His work. They are commissioned to proclaim the Gospel, demonstrate His love, and make disciples of all nations.

In verse 19, Jesus declares that He sanctifies Himself for the sake of His disciples' sanctification. He dedicates Himself wholly to God's will, setting an example for His followers. Through His sacrifice and obedience, they too can be sanctified in truth.

Finally, in verses 20, Jesus expands His prayer to include all future believers. He prays for the unity of all who would believe in Him through the message of His disciples. This unity mirrors the intimate relationship between Jesus and the Father, with believers being in both Jesus and the Father. Jesus desires this unity so that the world may recognize and believe that the Father sent Him.

Overall, in this passage, Jesus prays for His disciples' joy, protection from the evil one, sanctification, and unity with one another and with God. His prayer reveals His love and concern for His followers and underscores the mission and purpose He has given them in the world.

Unity Through Shared Glory

The glory which You have given Me I have given to them, that they may be one, just as We are one; I in them and You in Me, that they may be perfected in unity, so that the world may know that You sent Me, and loved them, even as You have loved Me.

John 17:22-23 is a verse from the New Testament of the Bible, specifically from the book of John. In this passage, Jesus is praying to God the Father shortly before his crucifixion. He speaks about the unity and glory that he shares with the Father, and how he desires to share that glory with his followers.

Let's break down the passage and explore its meaning:

"The glory which You have given Me I have given to them, that they may be one, just as We are one."

Jesus is referring to the glory that God the Father has bestowed upon him. He states that he has given this same glory to his disciples. By sharing his glory with them, Jesus intends to bring about a sense of unity among his followers. He desires that they become one, just as he and the Father are one. This unity is not merely physical or external but also implies a spiritual oneness and harmonious relationship among believers.

"I in them and You in Me, that they may be perfected in unity."

Jesus expresses his desire for a profound spiritual connection between himself, his disciples, and the Father. He wants to dwell within his followers and for the Father to dwell within him. This indwelling presence of Jesus and the Father in the disciples serves to unite them and help them grow in their faith. Through this unity and the presence of God in their lives, they can be perfected or brought to completion in their oneness.

"So that the world may know that You sent Me, and loved them, even as You have loved Me."

Jesus explains that the purpose of this unity and shared glory is to provide a visible witness to the world. When believers are united and display the love and glory of God, it serves as evidence that Jesus was sent by God and that God loves his disciples just as he loves Jesus himself. This testimony is intended to draw others to faith in Christ and to demonstrate the profound love of God for humanity.

In summary, John 17:22-23 highlights Jesus' desire for unity among his followers and his intention to share the glory and presence of God with them. This unity is meant to bring believers to completeness and serve as a testimony to the world of God's love and Jesus' divine mission.

Chapter 12

Jesus' desire for glory.

Father, I desire that they also, whom You have given Me, be with Me where I am, so that they may see My glory which You have given Me, for You loved Me before the foundation of the world. "O righteous Father, although the world has not known You, yet I have known You; and these have known that You sent Me; and I have made Your name known to them, and will make it known, so that the love with which You loved Me may be in them, and I in them."

In John 17:24-26, Jesus is praying to God the Father, expressing his desire for his followers to be with him and to experience his glory. He acknowledges that God loved him even before the world was created. Jesus refers to God as the righteous Father and acknowledges that while the world may not know God, he knows God and has made God's name known to his disciples. Jesus desires that the love with which God loved him may also be in his followers and that he himself may dwell within them.

This passage is part of Jesus' prayer during the Last Supper, where he intercedes for his disciples and all future believers. It reveals his deep love for his followers and his desire for them to share in his glory and experience the love of God.

By making God's name known to his disciples, Jesus is referring to the revelation of God's character, purpose, and truth. Throughout his ministry, Jesus taught his disciples about God, showed them God's love through his actions, and ultimately revealed God's plan for salvation through his own sacrifice on the cross.

Overall, these verses emphasize Jesus' intimate relationship with God the Father, his desire for his followers to know and experience that same love, and his commitment to making God's name known so that others may come to know and believe in God.

Chapter 18

Arrest in Garden

In the passage of John 18:1-11, several significant events take place during the arrest of Jesus in the garden of Gethsemane. Here's a breakdown of the key points:

Jesus and His disciples go to the garden: After speaking to His disciples, Jesus goes with them to the garden of Gethsemane, which is located near the Kidron Valley. This garden was a place where Jesus had often met with His disciples.

Judas leads a group to arrest Jesus: Judas, who had agreed to betray Jesus, arrives at the garden accompanied by a Roman cohort (a detachment of soldiers) and officers from the chief priests and Pharisees. They bring lanterns, torches, and weapons.

Jesus confronts the group: Jesus, aware of what is about to happen, steps forward and asks them, "Whom do you seek?" They respond by saying they are looking for Jesus of Nazareth.

Jesus reveals His identity: In response to their statement, Jesus declares, "I am He" (or "I am" in some translations). The power of His statement causes the group to draw back and fall to the ground, possibly overwhelmed by the presence and authority of Jesus.

Jesus protects His disciples: After the group regains composure, Jesus repeats His question, and they once again state they are seeking Jesus. In this instance, Jesus instructs them to let His disciples go and fulfill the words He had spoken previously, ensuring that none of His disciples would be lost.

Peter's impulsive action: Simon Peter, one of Jesus' disciples, draws a sword and strikes the high priest's slave, cutting off his right ear. The slave's name is mentioned as Malchus.

Jesus' response to Peter: Jesus instructs Peter to put his sword away and tells him that He must drink the cup the Father has given

Him. This statement indicates Jesus' acceptance of His impending arrest, suffering, and crucifixion as part of God's plan.

Overall, this passage highlights the courage and determination of Jesus to fulfill His mission despite knowing the challenges and suffering He would face. It also demonstrates Jesus' concern for His disciples' well-being, as He protects them from harm during His arrest.

John 18:12-24 Arrest, Peter's Denial

The passage you provided is from John 18:12-24 in the Bible, which describes the events following Jesus' arrest. Here's a breakdown of the key points:

After Jesus was arrested, He was bound and led to Annas first. Annas was the father-in-law of Caiaphas, who was the high priest that year. Annas was a former high priest himself and still held influence.

Simon Peter, one of Jesus' disciples, was following Him, along with another disciple who is not named in this passage. This unnamed disciple was known to the high priest, so he gained entry into the court of the high priest, while Peter stayed outside near the door.

The unnamed disciple spoke to the doorkeeper and brought Peter inside. While Peter was in the courtyard, a slave-girl who kept the door noticed him and questioned whether he was also one of Jesus' disciples. Peter denied it, saying, "I am not."

Meanwhile, the slaves and officers present had made a charcoal fire because it was cold, and they were warming themselves. Peter stood with them, warming himself as well.

The high priest then questioned Jesus about His disciples and His teaching. Jesus responded by stating that He had spoken openly to the world, teaching in synagogues and the temple where all Jews gathered. He questioned the need for the interrogation, suggesting that those who had heard Him should be questioned instead.

One of the officers standing nearby struck Jesus for His response to the high priest, criticizing the way He answered. Jesus defended Himself, saying that if He had spoken wrongly, they should testify to the wrong, but if He had spoken rightly, there was no reason to strike Him.

Annas then sent Jesus, still bound, to Caiaphas, the high priest.

This passage highlights the arrest of Jesus and the subsequent events involving Peter and the interrogation of Jesus by the high priest and his officers. It sets the stage for the trials and crucifixion of Jesus, which are described in further detail in the following chapters of the Gospel of John.

Pilate questions Jesus' authority.

In this passage from John 18:25-35, several events take place during Jesus' trial before Pilate.

Firstly, Peter, one of Jesus' disciples, is questioned by others who suspect he is associated with Jesus. They ask Peter if he is one of Jesus' disciples, to which he denies it twice, even when one of the slaves identifies him as someone who was in the garden with Jesus. After Peter's denial, a rooster crows, fulfilling Jesus' earlier prediction that Peter would deny him three times before the rooster crowed.

Meanwhile, Jesus is taken from Caiaphas, the high priest, to the Praetorium, which was the residence of the Roman governor, Pilate. It was early in the morning, and the Jewish authorities did not enter the Praetorium to avoid ceremonial defilement, so that they could eat the Passover meal. Instead, Pilate goes out to meet them and asks what accusation they bring against Jesus.

The Jewish authorities respond by saying that if Jesus were not an evildoer, they would not have brought him to Pilate. Pilate, not fully convinced, suggests that they take Jesus and judge him according to their own law. However, the Jewish authorities clarify that they do not have the authority to execute anyone, indicating that they wanted Pilate to pass the death sentence on Jesus.

Pilate then returns to the Praetorium and questions Jesus directly, asking if he is the King of the Jews. Jesus, in response, asks if Pilate is saying this on his own initiative or if others have told him about Jesus. Pilate replies, emphasizing that he is not Jewish and questions what Jesus has done to provoke the accusations made against him by the Jewish authorities.

Jesus' Kingdom Explained

Jesus answered, "My kingdom is not of this world. If My kingdom were of this world, then My servants would be fighting so that I would not be handed over to the Jews; but as it is, My kingdom is not of this realm." Therefore Pilate said to Him, "So You are a king?" Jesus answered, "You say correctly that I am a king. For this I have been born, and for this I have come into the world, to testify to the truth. Everyone who is of the truth hears My voice." Pilate said to Him, "What is truth?"

The conversation between Jesus and Pilate, as described in John 18:36-38, takes place during Jesus' trial before His crucifixion. In this exchange, Jesus explains that His kingdom is not of this world. He clarifies that if His kingdom were an earthly one, His followers would have fought to prevent His arrest by the Jewish authorities. However, Jesus emphasizes that His kingdom is not based on worldly power or politics.

Pilate, the Roman governor, then asks Jesus if He is a king. Jesus affirms that He is indeed a king, but He clarifies that His kingship is different from the earthly kingships Pilate might be familiar with. Jesus explains that His purpose in coming into the world is to bear witness to the truth. He states that those who belong to the truth will recognize His voice.

In response to Jesus' statement about truth, Pilate poses the question, "What is truth?" It is important to note that Pilate's question does not receive an explicit answer in the biblical account. The passage does not provide further dialogue between Jesus and

Pilate on this matter. Pilate's question reflects a philosophical inquiry into the nature of truth, which has been debated by scholars and thinkers throughout history.

While the Bible does not provide Jesus' direct response to Pilate's question, Christians generally believe that Jesus embodies the truth. In the Gospel of John, Jesus describes Himself as "the way, the truth, and the life" (John 14:6). Therefore, it can be understood that Jesus' life, teachings, and ultimately His sacrifice on the cross, serve as a revelation of truth and a means of salvation for humanity.

The question of "What is truth?" remains a profound and complex philosophical inquiry, beyond the scope of this biblical passage. It continues to be explored by scholars, philosophers, and individuals seeking understanding and knowledge.

Release Barabbas, Reject Jesus

And when he had said this, he went out again to the Jews and said to them, "I find no guilt in Him. But you have a custom that I release someone for you at the Passover; do you wish then that I release for you the King of the Jews?" So they cried out again, saying, "Not this Man, but Barabbas." Now Barabbas was a robber.

In the biblical passage you mentioned, John 18:38-40, it describes a dialogue between Pontius Pilate, the Roman governor of Judea, and the Jewish leaders regarding the fate of Jesus Christ. Pilate states that he finds no guilt in Jesus, implying that he does not believe Jesus deserves punishment or death.

However, Pilate acknowledges that it is the custom during the Passover festival to release a prisoner as an act of mercy. He offers the Jewish crowd a choice between releasing Jesus, whom he refers to as the "King of the Jews," or releasing Barabbas, who is described as a robber or criminal. The crowd responds by demanding the release of Barabbas instead of Jesus.

The choice of Barabbas over Jesus is significant and reflects the political and religious tensions of the time. It is believed that

Barabbas was involved in an insurrection or rebellion against Roman authority, and some scholars suggest that the crowd's preference for Barabbas may have been driven by their desire for a political Messiah who would lead them in a revolt against the Roman occupation.

The incident of Barabbas' release and Jesus' subsequent crucifixion is an essential part of the Christian narrative, symbolizing Jesus' sacrifice for humanity's sins and the choice between accepting him or rejecting him.

Chapter 19

Scourging of Jesus.

"Pilate then took Jesus and scourged Him".

John 19:1 is a verse from the New Testament of the Bible and it reads as follows in the New King James Version:

"Then Pilate took Jesus and scourged Him."

This verse describes an event that took place during the trial of Jesus before Pontius Pilate, the Roman governor of Judea. After Jesus was brought before Pilate, he was subjected to scourging or flogging, which was a form of punishment involving severe whipping with a multi-lashed whip. This act of scourging was a common practice in Roman judicial proceedings and often served as a prelude to crucifixion.

The Gospel accounts provide limited details about the actual scourging, but it is understood to be a brutal and painful ordeal. The purpose of the scourging was to humiliate and weaken the person being punished, often resulting in severe injuries and sometimes even death.

The verse you mentioned, John 19:1, is part of the narrative leading up to Jesus' crucifixion, which is a significant event in Christian theology, symbolizing Jesus' sacrifice for the redemption of humanity's sins.

Pilate's Fearful Interrogation

In the passage of John 19:2-10, we witness a crucial moment in the trial and condemnation of Jesus before His crucifixion. Let's break down the events and dialogue that took place:

The soldiers' actions: The Roman soldiers twisted together a crown of thorns and placed it on Jesus' head. They also dressed Him in a purple robe, intended to mock His claim of being a king. They approached Him, mocking and insulting Him by proclaiming, "Hail,

King of the Jews!" They further humiliated Him by slapping Him in the face.

Pilate's pronouncement of Jesus' innocence: Pilate, the Roman governor, came out and declared to the people that he found no guilt in Jesus. Pilate likely made this statement because he personally examined Jesus and could not find any basis for a charge against Him.

Jesus presented to the crowd: Pilate then presented Jesus, wearing the crown of thorns and the purple robe, to the crowd, saying, "Behold, the Man!" Pilate may have intended to evoke sympathy by showing the beaten and humiliated Jesus, emphasizing his innocence.

The crowd's demand for crucifixion: The chief priests and officers, representing the Jewish religious leadership, saw Jesus and demanded His crucifixion by shouting, "Crucify, crucify!" This indicates their intense opposition to Jesus and their desire to see Him executed.

Pilate's assertion of Jesus' innocence: Pilate responded to the crowd's demand by reiterating Jesus' innocence. He told them to take Jesus and crucify Him themselves, as he found no guilt in Him. Pilate may have been attempting to shift the responsibility to the Jewish authorities and avoid making a decision that could further escalate tensions.

The Jews' claim against Jesus: The Jewish leaders responded to Pilate, stating that according to their law, Jesus deserved to die because He had made Himself out to be the Son of God. By claiming to be the Son of God, Jesus was considered to be blaspheming under Jewish law, which carried a severe penalty.

Pilate's fear and questioning: Pilate became even more afraid upon hearing the Jews' claim that Jesus made Himself out to be the Son of God. He entered the Praetorium, the governor's official residence, and questioned Jesus, asking where He was from. However, Jesus did not provide an answer.

Pilate's reminder of his authority: Pilate, frustrated by Jesus' silence, reminded Him that he had the authority to release Him or to order His crucifixion. Pilate wanted Jesus to understand that his decision could determine Jesus' fate.

These verses highlight the growing tension surrounding Jesus' trial and the conflicting interests of the Jewish leaders, the Roman governor Pilate, and Jesus Himself. Ultimately, this dialogue leads to further deliberations and decisions that eventually result in Jesus being sentenced to crucifixion.

Pilate's Dilemma Jesus answered, "You would have no authority over Me, unless it had been given you from above; for this reason he who delivered Me to you has the greater sin." As a result of this Pilate made efforts to release Him, but the Jews cried out saying, "If you release this Man, you are no friend of Caesar; everyone who makes himself out to be a king opposes Caesar." Therefore when Pilate heard these words, he brought Jesus out, and sat down on the judgment seat at a place called The Pavement, but in Hebrew, Gabbatha. Now it was the day of preparation for the Passover; it was about the sixth hour. And he said to the Jews, "Behold, your King!" So they cried out, "Away with Him, away with Him, crucify Him!" Pilate said to them, "Shall I crucify your King?" The chief priests answered, "We have no king but Caesar."

The passage above is from the Gospel of John, specifically John 19:11-15. In this passage, Jesus is being questioned by Pontius Pilate, the Roman governor, during his trial before his crucifixion.

In response to Pilate's statement that he has the authority to crucify or release Jesus, Jesus declares that Pilate's authority comes from above, meaning it is ultimately given by God. Jesus implies that Pilate's power over him is part of God's plan and is ultimately under divine control.

Pilate recognizes that Jesus is innocent and tries to release him. However, the Jewish religious leaders, who had delivered Jesus to Pilate, opposed his release. They use political pressure, claiming that if Pilate releases Jesus, he is not a friend of Caesar, insinuating that Jesus is a threat to Roman authority by claiming to be a king.

Pilate brings Jesus out and presents him to the crowd, referring to him as their king. The crowd responds by demanding Jesus's crucifixion, shouting, "Away with Him, away with Him, crucify Him!" The chief priests, representing the Jewish religious establishment, respond by saying that they have no king but Caesar. This statement indicates their allegiance to the Roman authority rather than acknowledging Jesus as their king, which is a significant rejection of Jesus's messianic claims.

These events ultimately lead to Jesus's crucifixion, as Pilate succumbs to the pressure from the crowd and the Jewish leaders.

Crucifixion and Jesus' Words

The passage of John 19:16-30, describes the crucifixion of Jesus Christ. Here is a breakdown of the events mentioned:

Jesus is handed over to be crucified: After Pilate, the Roman governor, had Jesus scourged, he handed Him over to the soldiers to be crucified.

Jesus bears His own cross: Jesus carries His own cross to the place called Golgotha (meaning "Place of a Skull" in Hebrew).

Jesus is crucified with two others: At Golgotha, Jesus is crucified between two other men, one on either side.

Pilate's inscription: Pilate writes an inscription and puts it on the cross, which reads, "JESUS THE NAZARENE, THE KING OF THE JEWS." The inscription is written in Hebrew, Latin, and Greek so that many people can read it.

Dispute over the inscription: The chief priests of the Jews ask Pilate to change the wording of the inscription, but Pilate refuses, stating that what he has written will remain.

Soldiers divide Jesus' garments: The soldiers who crucify Jesus divide His outer garments among themselves. They also cast lots for His tunic, which was seamless and woven in one piece.

Jesus' mother and others at the cross: Standing near the cross are Jesus' mother, His mother's sister, Mary the wife of Clopas, and Mary Magdalene.

Jesus entrusts His mother to the disciple: Jesus, seeing His mother and the disciple whom He loved (often identified as John) standing nearby, asks His mother to consider the disciple as her son, and the disciple to consider His mother as his own. From that moment, the disciple takes Mary into his home.

Jesus declares, "I am thirsty": Jesus, aware that all things have been accomplished, says, "I am thirsty."

Jesus receives sour wine: A jar of sour wine is nearby, so the soldiers put a sponge full of the sour wine on a branch of hyssop and bring it to Jesus' mouth.

Jesus proclaims, "It is finished!": After receiving the sour wine, Jesus declares, "It is finished!" and then bows His head and gives up His spirit, signifying His death.

This passage recounts significant moments during the crucifixion of Jesus, including His interactions with those present and the fulfillment of Scripture.

Request to Remove Crucifixion Bodies

"Then the Jews, because it was the day of preparation, so that the bodies would not remain on the cross on the Sabbath (for that Sabbath was a high day), asked Pilate that their legs might be broken, and that they might be taken away".

John 19:31 is part of the account of the crucifixion of Jesus Christ in the New Testament. This verse describes a request made by the Jews to Pontius Pilate, the Roman governor, regarding the bodies of those who were crucified.

According to the verse, it was the day of preparation for the Sabbath, which means it was the day before the Sabbath. The Jews wanted to ensure that the bodies of those who were crucified would not remain on the crosses during the Sabbath day, as that would violate their religious laws and customs.

To expedite the removal of the bodies, the Jews asked Pilate to have the legs of the crucified individuals broken. Breaking their legs would accelerate their death by asphyxiation, as they would no longer be able to support themselves and breathe properly. This act would ensure that the bodies could be taken down from the crosses before the Sabbath began.

Breaking the legs of those being crucified was a common practice used by the Romans to hasten death. However, in the case of Jesus, when the soldiers came to break His legs, they found that He was already dead, so they did not break His legs. This fulfilled a prophecy from the Old Testament that none of His bones would be broken.

This event is significant in the context of the crucifixion narrative, highlighting the urgency to remove the bodies from the crosses before the Sabbath, and it also serves as a fulfillment of the prophecy regarding Jesus.

High Sabbath Urgency

"(for that Sabbath was a high day)",

John 19:31 is a verse from the Bible that appears in the Gospel of John, specifically in the context of the crucifixion and burial of Jesus Christ. The verse states:

"Now it was the day of Preparation, and the next day was to be a special Sabbath. Because the Jewish leaders did not want the bodies left on the crosses during the Sabbath, they asked Pilate to have the legs broken and the bodies taken down."

In this verse, the phrase "for that Sabbath was a high day" refers to the fact that the following day after Jesus' crucifixion was a special or high Sabbath. This particular Sabbath was of significant importance because it coincided with the annual Jewish festival of Passover. Passover is a major festival in the Jewish tradition, commemorating the Israelites' liberation from slavery in Egypt.

Observing the Sabbath was a key aspect of Jewish religious practice, and it involved refraining from work and engaging in worship and rest. The Jewish leaders wanted to ensure that the bodies of those crucified, including Jesus, were taken down from the crosses before the Sabbath began at sundown. Breaking the legs of the crucified individuals would hasten their death, allowing their bodies to be removed promptly.

By mentioning that the Sabbath was a high day, the Gospel of John emphasizes the significance of that particular Sabbath and the urgency to remove the bodies from the crosses before it began.

Burial of Jesus.

The passage of John 19:32-42, describes events that occurred after Jesus' crucifixion. Here's a breakdown of the key points:

The soldiers broke the legs of the two criminals crucified alongside Jesus, which was a common practice to hasten death.

When the soldiers came to Jesus, they noticed that He was already dead and, therefore, did not break His legs.

Instead, one of the soldiers pierced Jesus' side with a spear, and blood and water came out. This act fulfilled the Scriptures and served as a testimony.

Joseph of Arimathea, a disciple of Jesus who had kept his discipleship secret due to fear of the Jewish authorities, approached Pilate and requested permission to take Jesus' body.

Pilate granted permission, and Joseph, along with Nicodemus, another secret follower of Jesus, took Jesus' body.

Nicodemus brought a mixture of myrrh and aloes, weighing about a hundred pounds, to prepare the body for burial.

Jesus' body was wrapped in linen cloths along with the spices, following Jewish burial customs.

There was a garden near the crucifixion site, and within it, a new tomb where no one had been laid before.

They placed Jesus' body in the tomb because it was close by, and this took place on the Jewish day of preparation.

These events set the stage for Jesus' burial and subsequent resurrection, which is a central aspect of Christian belief and tradition.

Chapter 20

Mary Discovers Empty Tomb

Now on the first day of the week Mary Magdalene came early to the tomb, while it was still dark, and saw the stone already taken away from the tomb. So she ran and came to Simon Peter and to the other disciple whom Jesus loved, and said to them, "They have taken away the Lord out of the tomb, and we do not know where they have laid Him."

In the passage of John 20:1-2, it describes an event that took place on the first day of the week, which is traditionally known as Sunday. Mary Magdalene, one of Jesus' followers, went to the tomb early in the morning while it was still dark. When she arrived, she noticed that the stone covering the entrance of the tomb had been removed.

Seeing this, Mary ran to find Simon Peter and another disciple who is referred to as "the disciple whom Jesus loved," commonly believed to be the apostle John. Mary informed them that the body of Jesus had been taken from the tomb, and she did not know where it had been placed.

This passage sets the stage for the subsequent events described in the Gospel of John, where Peter and John rush to the tomb to verify Mary's claims and investigate the situation further. It leads into the discovery of the empty tomb and the appearances of Jesus to his disciples, which form an integral part of the resurrection narrative in Christian belief.

Tomb Discovery and Understanding

"So Peter and the other disciple went forth, and they were going to the tomb. The two were running together; and the other disciple ran ahead faster than Peter and came to the tomb first; and stooping and looking in, he saw the linen wrappings lying there; but he did not go in. And so Simon Peter also came, following him, and entered the tomb; and he saw the linen wrappings lying there, and the face-cloth which had been on His head, not lying with the linen wrappings, but rolled up in a place by itself. So the other disciple who had first come to the tomb then also entered, and he saw and believed. For as yet they did not understand the Scripture, that He must rise again from the dead. So the disciples went away again to their own homes".

In this passage from the Gospel of John (John 20:3-10), it describes an event that took place after the crucifixion of Jesus Christ. It involves two of Jesus' disciples, Peter and another disciple who is often referred to as the "beloved disciple" or the "disciple whom Jesus loved."

According to the passage, Peter and the other disciple went to the tomb where Jesus had been buried. The other disciple, who was faster, reached the tomb first and looked inside. He saw the linen wrappings that had been used to bury Jesus but did not enter the tomb. Peter arrived shortly after and went inside the tomb. He also saw the linen wrappings lying there, as well as a separate cloth that had been used to cover Jesus' face. The face-cloth was not with the linen wrappings but was rolled up in a place by itself.

Then, the other disciple also entered the tomb, and upon seeing the linen wrappings and the face-cloth, he believed. However, the passage states that neither Peter nor the other disciple fully understood at that moment that Jesus had risen from the dead, even though the Scripture had foretold it. After this encounter, the disciples went back to their own homes.

This passage is significant because it highlights the different reactions and actions of Peter and the other disciple upon finding the empty tomb. It also emphasizes that their understanding of the resurrection was not yet complete, and they needed further revelations and experiences to grasp the full significance of Jesus' resurrection.

Mary encounters resurrected Jesus.

The passage from the Gospel of John, specifically John 20:11-18 describes an encounter between Mary Magdalene and Jesus after His resurrection.

In the story, Mary Magdalene is standing outside the tomb where Jesus had been buried. She is grieving and weeping for His loss. As she looks into the tomb, she sees two angels in white sitting where Jesus' body had been lying. The angels ask her why she is weeping, and she responds by saying that someone has taken away her Lord, and she doesn't know where they have laid Him.

After saying this, Mary turns around and sees Jesus standing there, but she doesn't recognize Him. Jesus asks her why she is weeping and whom she is seeking. Thinking He is the gardener, she asks Him if He knows where the body of Jesus has been taken, and she promises to take care of it.

Then, Jesus calls her by name, saying, "Mary!" At that moment, she realizes it is Jesus. She responds to Him in Hebrew, saying, "Rabboni!" which means "Teacher." Jesus tells her not to cling to Him because He has not yet ascended to the Father. Instead, He instructs her to go to His disciples, His brethren, and tell them that He is ascending to His Father and their Father, to His God and their God.

Mary Magdalene goes to the disciples and announces, "I have seen the Lord!" She shares with them the message that Jesus had given her.

This passage is significant because it shows Mary Magdalene as one of the first witnesses to Jesus' resurrection. It also highlights the personal and intimate encounter she had with Jesus, where He calls her by name and reveals Himself to her. Mary's response to this encounter demonstrates her deep love and devotion to Jesus, as well as her role in spreading the news of His resurrection to the disciples.

In this passage from the Gospel of John 20:19-29 , the events take place after Jesus' resurrection. The disciples are gathered together in a room with the doors shut, out of fear of the Jewish authorities. Suddenly, Jesus appears among them, despite the closed doors, and greets them with the words, "Peace be with you."

Jesus then shows them His hands and His side, which bear the scars of His crucifixion. The disciples rejoice upon seeing the Lord. Jesus repeats His greeting of peace and declares that just as the Father had sent Him, He now sends them. After saying this, Jesus breathes on them and imparts the Holy Spirit to them, empowering them for their mission.

Jesus tells the disciples that if they forgive anyone's sins, those sins are forgiven, and if they retain anyone's sins, they are retained. This indicates that the disciples are given the authority to proclaim the forgiveness of sins in Jesus' name.

However, Thomas, one of the twelve disciples, was not present when Jesus appeared. When the other disciples tell him about seeing the Lord, Thomas expresses skepticism and says that he would need physical proof before believing. He states that unless he sees the marks of the nails in Jesus' hands and puts his hand into Jesus' side, he will not believe.

Eight days later, the disciples are gathered again, and Thomas is with them this time. Once again, Jesus appears among them, even though the doors are shut, and greets them with peace. Jesus then turns to Thomas and invites him to touch His wounds and see for himself. Overwhelmed by this evidence, Thomas exclaims, "My Lord and my God!"

Jesus acknowledges Thomas' belief but also blesses those who will believe in Him without physically seeing Him. This statement extends to future generations who will come to believe in Jesus through the testimony of others, without having the opportunity to see Him in person.

This passage highlights the importance of faith in Jesus' resurrection and the role of the disciples in carrying out His mission, empowered by the Holy Spirit. It

Faith in Resurrection & Testimony

Jesus acknowledges Thomas' belief but also blesses those who will believe in Him without physically seeing Him. This statement extends to future generations who will come to believe in Jesus through the testimony of others, without having the opportunity to see Him in person.

This passage highlights the importance of faith in Jesus' resurrection and the role of the disciples in carrying out His mission, empowered by the Holy Spirit. It shows that Jesus recognizes the struggle that some may have in believing in His resurrection without physical proof. Thomas, one of the disciples, famously doubted the resurrection until he personally saw and touched Jesus' wounds.

However, Jesus goes beyond acknowledging Thomas' belief and emphasizes the significance of faith for future generations. He blesses those who will come to believe in Him without physically seeing Him. This statement implies that faith is not solely reliant on tangible evidence but is a spiritual conviction that transcends physical limitations.

Jesus anticipates that there will be people in the future who will believe in Him through the testimony and witness of others. This highlights the role of the disciples and subsequent followers of Jesus in sharing the good news of His resurrection. Their witness becomes instrumental in leading others to faith, as they provide the accounts and teachings of Jesus, even though they did not physically witness the events themselves.

Additionally, Jesus promises to send the Holy Spirit to empower the disciples in their mission to spread the message of His resurrection. This divine presence will work through them, enabling them to fulfill their calling and strengthen the faith of those who come to believe.

Overall, this passage underscores the importance of faith in Jesus' resurrection and the role of believers in sharing the Gospel with future generations. It emphasizes that belief in Jesus is not solely dependent on seeing Him physically but can be cultivated through the testimony and witness of others, supported by the empowering presence of the Holy Spirit.

Belief in Jesus for Life.

"Therefore many other signs Jesus also performed in the presence of the disciples, which are not written in this book; but these have been written so that you may believe that Jesus is the Christ, the Son of God; and that believing you may have life in His name".

John 20:30-31 is a passage from the Bible, specifically from the Gospel of John. In these verses, John explains the purpose behind writing his Gospel account. Let's break down the passage:

"Therefore many other signs Jesus also performed in the presence of the disciples, which are not written in this book."

This line acknowledges that Jesus performed many other miraculous signs in the presence of His disciples, which are not recorded in the Gospel of John. John is aware that his Gospel account does not include all the miracles Jesus performed during His ministry.

"But these have been written so that you may believe that Jesus is the Christ, the Son of God."

John states that the purpose of his writing is to provide evidence and testimony so that readers may come to believe that Jesus is the Messiah (the Christ) and the Son of God. John's Gospel presents Jesus as the divine Son of God, emphasizing His deity and the significance of His ministry.

"And that believing you may have life in His name."

John concludes by expressing his desire for readers to believe in Jesus and have life through Him. The belief in Jesus as the Christ and the Son of God is not merely intellectual assent but a personal trust and reliance that brings eternal life. John's Gospel emphasizes the concept of eternal life and the importance of faith in Jesus as the means to receive it.

In summary, John's purpose in writing his Gospel account is to present the signs and testimonies that lead to faith in Jesus as the Christ, the Son of God, and to encourage readers to believe in Him so that they may have eternal life.

Chapter 21

Jesus' Post-Resurrection Encounter

In John 21:1-11, the passage describes an encounter between Jesus and some of His disciples after His resurrection. The disciples, including Simon Peter, Thomas, Nathanael, the sons of Zebedee (James and John), and two others, were gathered together at the Sea of Tiberias (also known as the Sea of Galilee).

Simon Peter, expressing a desire to go fishing, was accompanied by the other disciples. They spent the entire night fishing but caught nothing. As day broke, Jesus appeared on the beach, although the disciples did not recognize Him at first.

Jesus called out to them, referring to them as "children" and asked if they had caught any fish. They replied that they had not. Jesus then instructed them to cast their net on the right side of the boat, assuring them that they would find a catch. Following His guidance, the disciples cast their net and were unable to haul it in due to the abundance of fish.

At this point, the disciple whom Jesus loved (traditionally identified as the apostle John) recognized that it was Jesus standing on the shore. He told Peter, who immediately put on his outer garment (he had stripped down for work) and jumped into the sea to reach Jesus.

The rest of the disciples, in the small boat, dragged the net full of fish toward the shore, which was about one hundred yards away. Once on land, they discovered a charcoal fire already prepared, with fish and bread on it.

Jesus then asked the disciples to bring some of the fish they had caught. Simon Peter went to the net and pulled it to the shore. Surprisingly, even though the catch was large, consisting of 153 large fish, the net did not tear.

This passage signifies a significant encounter between Jesus and His disciples following His resurrection. It serves as a confirmation of His identity and authority, as well as a demonstration of His care for His disciples' needs. The miraculous catch of fish and the provision of food further reinforce Jesus' role as the provider and sustainer of His followers.

Jesus' Questions to Peter

In this passage from John 21:12-17, Jesus appears to His disciples after His resurrection and invites them to have breakfast with Him. The disciples recognized that it was Jesus and did not question His identity. Jesus took bread and fish and gave them to the disciples to eat, demonstrating His physical presence with them.

After breakfast, Jesus engaged in a conversation with Simon Peter. He asked Peter three times if he loved Him, and each time Peter affirmed his love for Jesus. The repetition of the question and Peter's response may have been significant, highlighting the significance of Peter's love and commitment to Jesus.

In response to Peter's declaration of love, Jesus gave him a command. The first two times, Jesus told Peter to "tend My lambs" and "shepherd My sheep," emphasizing his responsibility to care for and guide the followers of Jesus. The third time, Jesus again asked Peter if he loved Him, and Peter affirmed his love once more. Jesus then instructed him to "tend My sheep," reiterating his role in shepherding and nurturing the believers.

This exchange between Jesus and Peter carries symbolic meaning. It signifies Jesus' reaffirmation of Peter's role as a leader among the disciples and in the early Christian community. It also emphasizes the importance of love and care in shepherding others and serving God's people.

Overall, this passage illustrates Jesus' post-resurrection appearance to His disciples, His recognition by the disciples, His act of sharing a meal with them, and His specific conversation with Peter about love and responsibility.

Peter's Martyrdom and John

John 21:18-25 from the New Testament of the Bible. In this passage, Jesus is speaking to the disciple Peter. He tells Peter that when he was younger, he used to dress himself and go wherever he wanted, but when he grows old, he will be led by others and taken to places he may not want to go. Jesus is indicating that Peter would die a martyr's death, glorifying God through his death.

After Jesus speaks these words to Peter, Peter notices another disciple following them, described as the disciple whom Jesus loved. This disciple is often believed to be John, the author of the Gospel of John. Peter asks Jesus about the fate of this disciple, to which Jesus responds by saying that if He wants this disciple to remain until He comes again, it should not concern Peter. Jesus instructs Peter to focus on following Him.

The passage clarifies that a saying had spread among the believers that the disciple whom Jesus loved would not die. However, the passage emphasizes that Jesus did not actually say that the disciple would not die, but rather pointed out that it was not Peter's concern. The passage concludes by stating that the disciple who is testifying to these things and wrote the Gospel of John is the one providing this account, and that his testimony is considered true. Additionally, it mentions that there are many other things that Jesus did which are not recorded in detail, suggesting that the world itself would not be able to contain all the books that could be written about Jesus' actions.

This passage provides insights into the relationship between Jesus and his disciples, particularly focusing on Peter and the disciple whom Jesus loved, commonly believed to be John. It also highlights the acceptance of different roles and destinies among the disciples and emphasizes the importance of following Jesus.

Ingram Content Group UK Ltd.
Milton Keynes UK
UKHW010637050623
422889UK00001B/165